REFERENCE

ENGLISH
SKILL
BUILDER

JACK E. HULBERT, Ph.D.

Professor of Business Education
and Administrative Services
School of Business and Economics
North Carolina A & T State University,

SOUTH-WESTERN PUBLISHING CO.

Senior Developmental Editor: Carol Lynne Ruhl
Acquisitions Editor: Janie F. Schwark
Production Editor: Nancy Shockey
Senior Designer: Jim DeSollar
Marketing Manager: Al S. Roane
Consulting Editor: Elizabeth Ackley

ISBN: 0-538-61667-9

2 3 4 5 6 7 D 98 97 96 95 94 93 92

Printed in the United States of America

ENGLISH SKILL BUILDER REFERENCE MANUAL

Table of Contents

Nouns

Definition:
A **noun** is the name of a person, place, thing, event, or idea.

| | | | Events/ | |
Persons	**Places**	**Things**	**Activities**	**Ideas**
editor	house	bench	race	democracy
employer	store	car	picnic	freedom
manager	lake	trunk	sale	dream
attorney	stage	envelope	contest	courage
author	valley	telephone	party	loyalty

FORMS OF NOUNS

A **singular noun** refers to one item. A **plural noun** refers to more than one item.

Nouns can have two cases: possessive and general. The **possessive case** indicates ownerships and similar relationships. The **general case** is simply a noun that does not involve ownership.

Here are examples of these four forms. Any word that can have these forms is a noun.

| General Case | | Possessive Case | |
Singular	**Plural**	**Singular**	**Plural**
employee	employees	employee's	employees'
client	clients	client's	clients'
division	divisions	division's	divisions'
customer	customers	customer's	customers'
computer	computers	computer's	computers'

SPELLING REGULAR NOUN PLURALS

Noun plurals are generally formed in one of the following two ways:

1. By adding *-s* if the singular noun ends in any sound *other than* a hissing sound like *s* or *z* (spelled *s, ss, z, ch, sh,* or *x*).

Singular	Plural
book	books
plant	plants
place	places
mile	miles

2. By adding *-es* if the singular noun ends in a hissing sound.

Singular	Plural
tax	taxes
blitz	blitzes
glass	glasses
dish	dishes
match	matches

    Exception: If the noun ends in *o* preceded by a consonant, *-es* is usually added, unless the noun relates to music.

potato	potatoes
piano	pianos
solo	solos

SPELLING IRREGULAR NOUN PLURALS

Some nouns have irregular plurals.

1. For most nouns ending in *fe*, change the *f* to *v* before adding *-s*. For most nouns ending in *f*, change the *f* to *v* before adding *-es*.

Singular	Plural	Singular	Plural
life	lives	shelf	shelves
knife	knives	leaf	leaves
wife	wives	loaf	loaves

2. For nouns ending in *y* preceded by a consonant, change the *y* to *i* before adding *-es*. For nouns ending in *y* preceded by a vowel, add *-s* without changing the *y*.

Singular	Plural	Singular	Plural
apology	apologies	boy	boys
authority	authorities	attorney	attorneys
assembly	assemblies	ray	rays

3. A few nouns do not add *-s* or *-es* to form the plural but change their spelling.

Singular	Plural
foot	feet
goose	geese
ox	oxen
man	men
stepchild	stepchildren

4. A few nouns borrowed from foreign languages keep their foreign plural spellings. Others have acquired new English forms in addition to their original ones.

Singular	Plural
datum/data	data
curriculum	curriculums/curricula
crisis	crises
agenda	agendas
stimulus	stimuli
appendix	appendixes/appendices
analysis	analyses
criterion	criteria
bacterium	bacteria

5. A few nouns, mostly naming fields of study, are plural in spelling but singular in use.

physics	electronics
news	mathematics
economics	

6. A few nouns, mostly species of animals, use the same spelling for singular and plural number. Only the context (surrounding language) indicates which number the writer intends. Use an up-to-date dictionary for correct spellings when you are uncertain.

deer	sheep
moose	species
series	

CHECK YOUR UNDERSTANDING 2

Give the plural spelling of each of the following nouns. Explain all differences between the spellings of the singular and plural forms.

belief	county	patch	sheep
dish	key	base	child
stereo	potato	tomato	package
lady	wife	agency	criterion
attorney	analysis	mathematics	soprano

FORMING THE POSSESSIVE CASE OF SINGULAR NOUNS

1. To form the possessive case of any singular noun, add an apostrophe and -s to the singular noun.

Singular General Case	Singular Possessive Case
friend	friend's dress
brother	brother's car
officer	officer's badge
chef	chef's recipe
author	author's book

2. If a singular noun ends in an s-like sound and has two or more syllables, omit the s after the apostrophe to make the noun possessive.

> Ms. Perkins' article
> Mr. Adams' investment
> goodness' sake

Exception: Include the s if you expect the sound to be pronounced.

> the mattress's firmness   the cutlass's blade

FORMING THE POSSESSIVE CASE OF PLURAL NOUNS

1. To form the possessive case of plural nouns ending in *s*, add an apostrophe *after* the *s*.

Plural General Case	Plural Possessive Case
customers	customers' response
companies	companies' employees
students	students' papers
ladies	ladies' accessories

2. To form the possessive case of plural nouns that do not end in *s*, add an apostrophe and *-s*.

Plural General Case	Plural Possessive Case
feet	feet's aches
mice	mice's food
alumni	alumni's reunion
women	women's briefcases
stepchildren	stepchildren's goals

OF PHRASES

You may express ownership and similar relationships with an *of* phrase as well as with a noun in possessive case. Possessive case is more concise, but an *of* phrase puts greater emphasis on the noun naming the "owner." When you use a noun in possessive case, use an *of* phrase to determine whether singular or plural number is appropriate. If the "owner" is singular in the *of* phrase, use the possessive case, singular number. If the "owner" is plural in the *of* phrase, use the possessive case, plural number.

Of Phrase	Possessive Case
car of the girl	girl's car
cars of the girls	girls' cars
clothes of the actress	actress's clothes
clothes of the actresses	actresses' clothes
report of the treasurer	treasurer's report
reports of the treasurers	treasurers' reports
offer of the buyer	buyer's offer
offers of the buyers	buyers' offers
paving of the driveway	driveway's paving

Note: Generally use an *of* phrase when inanimate (nonliving) items are used in possessive form.

CHECK YOUR UNDERSTANDING 3

Give the singular possessive form and the plural possessive form for each of the following nouns:

group	dog	grandchild	committee
company	dollar	year	writer
brother	woman	calf	executive

SPECIAL USES INVOLVING POSSESSIVES

Follow these rules for special uses involving possessives:

1. Joint Ownership—To show that two or more persons own the same thing, add an apostrophe and *-s* to the last name only.

    Betty and *Sasha's* computer has two disk drives.
    Mathis and *Irby's* profit for last year was large.

2. Separate Ownership—To show that *each* of the persons owns something, add *'s* to each owner's name.

    Betty's and *Sasha's* computers have two disk drives.
    Mathis's and *Irby's* profits for last year were large.

CHECK YOUR UNDERSTANDING 4

Select the correct possessive form in each of the following sentences:

1. (Nancy and Jim's, Nancy's and Jim's) mother took the team members to the contest.
2. We bought the material at (Wade's & Taylor's, Wade & Taylor's) fabric store.
3. Was your (sister-in-laws', sister-in-law's) accident serious?
4. Mr. (Hamptons', Hampton's) and Mr. (Jacksons', Jackson's) opinions are respected.
5. The (auditors', auditor's) certificate and the (accountants', accountant's) certificate were from the same university.

PROPER AND COMMON NOUNS

A **proper noun** is the specific name of a particular person, place, or thing; group, organization, or institution; historical period or event; calendar unit or holiday. Capitalize the initial letters of the proper noun (except for minor words).

A **common noun** is a general name used to refer to any member of a class of persons, places, things, events, or ideas.

The words in the left column are common nouns that could be used to refer to the proper nouns in the right column.

Common Nouns (General)	Proper Nouns (Specific Name)
vocalist, entertainer, female	Barbara Mandrell
metropolitan area	Dallas
building; natural; displays of animals, birds, and insects	Museum of Natural History
concrete wall, dam	Hoover Dam
capital, city	Denver
athlete, tennis, winner	Billie Jean King
holiday, celebration	Thanksgiving Day

CHECK YOUR UNDERSTANDING 5

Write three proper nouns named by each of the following common nouns:

city	university	holiday	car
company	building	singer	day

Write two common nouns that could be used in reference to these proper nouns.

Glacier National Park	General Motors
Paul Newman	Department of Defense
Vietnam Memorial	*Gone with the Wind*

COLLECTIVE NOUNS

Collective nouns are nouns whose singular form names a group of individuals.

association	union	orchestra	administration
department	crew	league	mob
class	club	company	circle (of friends)
gang	majority	crowd	minority

1. Collective nouns can refer to a group as a unit or to the individual members of a group. When a collective noun refers to a group as a unit, the collective noun requires a singular verb and pronoun.

    The *committee is* meeting this afternoon to make *its* decision.

2. When a collective noun refers to the individual members of a group, the collective noun requires a plural verb and pronoun.

The *committee are* evaluating numerous applications, and *they* will make *their* decisions by Friday. (The members act as individuals as they evaluate.)

CHECK YOUR UNDERSTANDING 6

Select the collective nouns from the following list of nouns:

sofa	accountant	staff	orchestra	grass
faculty	class	book	jury	council
house	pen	board (as in board of directors)	girl	paper

CONCRETE AND ABSTRACT NOUNS

Concrete nouns name things that you can touch, see, hear, smell, or taste. For example, the nouns *persons*, *places*, *things*, *events*, and *activities*, as well as the nouns that could be listed under such headings, are concrete nouns. You can classify some nouns under more than one of these headings.

Persons	Places	Things	Events/Activities
employer	street	newspaper	track meet
artist	yard	bed	conference
teacher	auditorium	table	contest
student	house	stove	race
salesperson	building	suit	regatta
driver	restaurant	computer	seminar
male	store	pencil	class
photographer	garage	telephone	game

Abstract nouns name ideas, qualities, and conditions. Thus, abstract nouns name what cannot be observed or perceived directly. While you can observe examples of honesty, you cannot feel, see, touch, hear, or smell *honesty*.

Abstract nouns are often based on adjectives and name the quality described by that adjective. (See Section D for information about adjectives.) For example, the abstract noun *goodness* is based on the adjective *good*. Abstract nouns can be based on other parts of speech, too. For example, the abstract noun *cooperation* is based on the verb *cooperate*. (See Section C for information about verbs.)

Base Word	Abstract Noun
feel	feeling
concrete	concreteness
simple	simplicity
willing	willingness
patient	patience
assist	assistance
friend	friendship

Use concrete nouns whenever possible. Concrete nouns help make messages clear and forceful.

CHECK YOUR UNDERSTANDING 7

List each of the following nouns under the heading "Concrete" or "Abstract".

dictionary	excellence	tolerance	door
intelligence	floor	friendship	ability
picture	cabinet	fence	fairness

COMPOUND NOUNS

Compound nouns are two nouns or a noun and other parts of speech combined to name one thing. You may write compound nouns as one single word, as separate words, or as hyphenated words. When in doubt, check an up-to-date dictionary.

Single Word	Separate Words	Hyphenated Words
taxpayer	branch office	member-at-large
businessperson	shopping center	runner-up
blueprint	high school	president-elect

Note: To make a separated or hyphenated compound noun plural, make the *main* word plural.

Singular	Plural
mother-in-law	mothers-in-law
vice president	vice presidents
notary public	notaries public

CHECK YOUR UNDERSTANDING 8

Write the following compound nouns correctly:

civil service	business person
attorney general	post office
drive in	get together
lay out	micro computer
brother in law	home owner

EDITING APPLICATIONS

1. Revise the following sentences, correcting any noun errors.

    Example: One of the member's gives a large contribution each year.

    Revision: One of the *members* gives a large contribution each year.

    a. Encourage childrens interest in reading.
    b. The stockholders' received dividends this year.
    c. Susan Monroe's father works with four other attornies.
    d. Mathematics is an essential course in any curricula.
    e. You can buy computer disks at Tom's and Mary store.
    f. The residents of those three countys will vote next Tuesday.
    g. Mr. Caracas's leaves Saturday on a three-week business trip.
    h. The baked potatoes' were served with large steaks.
    i. They sell that sweater in the mens store on Dayton Avenue.
    j. You will need to get permission from Mary and Alice's mothers.
    k. He spent a weeks' salary to buy a new sofa.
    l. She will attend the board of directors meeting.
    m. The leafs begin to fall in September.
    n. John attended the meeting with three other secretarys.
    o. The jury have been disagreeing for two day.
    p. Many lifes are extended through improved health care.
    q. The committee member unanimously agreed to buy the equipment.
    r. Bryan Stanton's daughter in law is an officer of Central State Bank.
    s. The music teacher said he needs five alto for the concert.
    t. These bacterium are causing many illnesses.

2. Revise the sentences on page 11 by replacing each *of* phrase by a possessive noun with the same meaning.

Example: The report of the committee was well written.
Revision: The *committee's* report was well written.

a.   The reputation of the company is outstanding.
b.   The receipts of the customer will verify the numerous purchases.
c.   Attitudes of people affect many relationships.
d.   The voice of a sales representative is important in business.
e.   The decision of the judge was fair.

3.   Revise the following sentences by replacing each possessive noun with an *of* phrase with the same meaning.

Example: The receipts should be taken to the supervisor's office.
Revision: The receipts should be taken to the office *of the supervisor.*

a.   It is everyone's responsibility to participate.
b.   We used your student's ideas to prepare the ad.
c.   The authorities' actions were entirely legal.
d.   The manager's report was well written.
e.   The committee's chairperson demonstrated excellent leadership skills.

4.   In each of the following sentences identify the concrete nouns and the abstract nouns.

Example: The girls wrote a paper on democracy.
 Answer: concrete nouns—girls, paper
abstract nouns—democracy

a.   The members of the organization will appreciate your assistance.
b.   Her uncle is an executive in a Dallas bank.
c.   A musical concert will be held in the auditorium.
d.   Susan values her friendship and is happy that Mary is her neighbor.
e.   Her employer recommended her promotion because of her performance.

5.   Write the plural and plural possessive forms for the singular words listed below.

Example:	*Singular*	*Plural*	*Plural Possessive*
	lady	ladies	ladies'

a.   attorney
b.   alto
c.   secretary

      d. wife
      e. sheet
      f. father-in-law
      g. child
      h. company
      i. alumna
      j. week

SECTION B

Pronouns

> **Definition:**
> A **pronoun** is a word that can be substituted for a noun.

Nouns	Pronouns
Bill Johnson	he
Mrs. Barton	she
the table	it
Miss Daukworth and Mrs. Wade	they
students in class	you
a person	someone
any person	anybody

There are several kinds of pronouns. In business messages, however, personal pronouns are by far the most frequently used and most important.

PERSONAL PRONOUNS

Personal pronouns are divided into three categories: first person, second person, and third person.

First-person personal pronouns can replace the name of the speaker.

My name is *Ann Jacobs. I* am your sales representative.

Second-person personal pronouns can replace the name of the person addressed.

> *You* may proceed with the project.

Third-person personal pronouns can replace the name of the person or thing spoken about.

> *Mr. Kenn Finley* completed *his* degree. *He* will now enter medical school.

Third-person personal pronouns include feminine, masculine, and neuter genders. The **masculine** forms refer to males. The **feminine** forms refer to females. The **neuter** forms refer to inanimate objects and animals.

Feminine	Masculine	Neuter
she	he	it

Cases of Personal Pronouns

As shown in Table B-1 on page 14, personal pronouns have three cases.

1. Subjective case—used when the personal pronoun is a subject or a predicate noun (For definitions, see Section J of the Reference Division.)
2. Objective case—used when the personal pronoun is a direct object, indirect object, or object of a preposition (For definitions, see Section J of the Reference Division.)
3. Possessive case—used to show ownership

In addition, personal pronouns form compounds with *-self/-selves*. These are called *reflexive pronouns* when used as objects. They are called *intensive pronouns* when used to emphasize a preceding noun or pronoun.

> Steven hurt *himself* when he fell off the ladder. (reflexive)
> I *myself* will grade the test papers. (intensive)

Pronoun/Antecedent Agreement

An **antecedent** is a noun which a pronoun replaces. A pronoun substituting for a noun must agree in person, number, and gender with that noun. For example, a pronoun replacing the name of a woman must be third person, singular in number, and feminine in gender.

Determine the *case* of the pronoun by the way you use the pronoun in the sentence.

> *Julie* drove *her* brother to the airport.

If any other personal pronoun were substituted for *her* in this example, an agreement error would result. The sentence would be incoherent.

TABLE B-1	SUMMARY OF PERSONAL PRONOUNS				
	Subjective Case	Objective Case	Possessive Case Used with a Noun	Possessive Case Used without a Noun	Reflexive and Intensive Forms
First-Person Singular	I	me	my	mine	myself
First-Person Plural	we	us	our	ours	ourselves
Second-Person Singular	you	you	your	yours	yourself
Second-Person Plural	you	you	your	yours	yourselves
Third-Person Singular	she	her	her	hers	herself
	he	him	his	his	himself
	it	it	its	its	itself
Third-Person Plural	they	them	their	theirs	themselves

CHECK YOUR UNDERSTANDING 9

In each of the following sentences, select the appropriate personal pronoun. Be prepared to explain the form you select.

Example: Ms. Kinney surprised (herself, her—referring to Ms. Kinney) when she made the highest grade on the test.

Revision: Ms. Kinney surprised *herself* when she made the highest grade on the test.

1. Mae confirmed the dates with (he, him—referring to Mr. Lamply) and (she, her—referring to Mrs. Colt).
2. The agreement was between the attorney and (he, him).
3. (He, him) prepared the report for the sales meeting.
4. The library materials were reserved for Thomas and (he, him—referring to Doug.)
5. Mr. Kesler proved to (him, himself—referring to Mr. Kesler) that he could improve his reading skill.

6. Do you think that it was (she, her)?
7. Collins and Company hired two men and (I, me) last week.
8. Joey hurt (hisself, himself) when he fell off the bicycle.
9. The person who will file the reports is (she, her).
10. John (himself, hisself) will take the samples to the meeting.

Singular or Plural Pronouns with Collective Nouns

Use singular pronouns to refer to a collective noun treated as a unit.

The jury gave its verdict.

Use plural pronouns to refer to a collective noun if the members of the group act separately.

The class have completed their projects.

CHECK YOUR UNDERSTANDING 10

Identify the appropriate personal pronoun to complete each of the following sentences.

1. The faculty have planned _____ vacations.
2. The audience is showing _____ approval.
3. The committee are expressing _____ differences.
4. The company buys _____ supplies locally.
5. The family gave _____ contribution to the scholarship fund.

INTERROGATIVE PRONOUNS

Interrogative pronouns (*who, which, what*) are used to ask questions. The interrogative pronoun *who* has three case forms: subjective, objective, and possessive.

Subjective Case

Who sold a painting?
Whoever would buy a house without inspecting it?

Objective Case

To whom shall I give the package?
Whomever did he call at 2:00 a.m.?

Possessive Case

Whose idea was discussed? (Note: The possessive form *whose* has no apostrophe. *Who's* is the contraction of *who is*.)

Use the interrogative pronouns *which* and *what* to ask other kinds of questions. These pronouns have the same form in all uses.

As Subject	**As Object**
Which was ordered?	*What* did she lose?
What broke the window?	To *which* did they respond?

RELATIVE PRONOUNS

Relative pronouns introduce clauses that modify nouns. Three common relative pronouns are *who*, *which*, and *that*. *Who* is used to refer to people and has three case forms: subjective, objective, and possessive.

Subjective Case

The person *who* wrote the article is Jeff.
A speaker *who* is confident will usually do a good job.
Whoever wins the contest will provide outstanding leadership.

Objective Case

The students *whom* we have sponsored have excelled in their studies.
Mrs. Morrow will transfer the money to *whomever* you suggest.

Possessive Case

The woman *whose* car was damaged is Ellen's aunt.

The relative pronouns *which* and *that* have the same form in all uses. *Which* is used to refer to things while *that* is used to refer to people or things. Most clauses introduced by *which* are set off with commas because the clauses are unnecessary to the meaning of the sentence. Clauses that are necessary to the meaning of the sentence will begin with *that*.

The analysis sheets, *which* you prepared yesterday, are in Brian's office.
The building *that* he bought will be available for occupancy next month.

INDEFINITE PRONOUNS

Indefinite pronouns do not have specific antecedents.

one	each	every	no one
someone	anyone	everyone	nobody
somebody	anybody	everybody	nothing
something	anything	everything	none/some
either	neither	many	

Most indefinite pronouns are singular in form. However, *none* and *some* may be singular or plural in form. If *none* and *some* are followed by singular words, consider them singular. If followed by plural words, consider them plural.

> None of the *money* is missing.
> Some of the *basketball players* are absent today.

Indefinite pronouns are similar to nouns. Form the possessive case of these pronouns by adding *'s* to the singular pronoun.

someone's	anyone's	everyone's
somebody's	anybody's	everybody's

CHECK YOUR UNDERSTANDING 11

List the indefinite pronouns in the following sentences:

1. Everyone has contributed to the food fund.
2. Mr. Grady said that professionals will do some of the decorating.
3. She agreed that anyone who has been with the firm for ten years is eligible.
4. The manager congratulated everybody for doing an excellent job.
5. Did anybody speak to Paula while she was waiting to buy tickets?

EDITING APPLICATIONS

1. Revise the following sentences, replacing the underlined expression with the appropriate personal pronoun.

   Example: The store encourages <u>the store's</u> employees to be courteous.

   Revision: The store encourages <u>its</u> employees to be courteous.

   a. The secretary read <u>the members'</u> names quickly.
   b. Miss Lewis promised <u>Miss Lewis</u> that she would walk two miles every day.

    c. We asked <u>the man in the car</u> for directions.

    d. <u>The lady at the information desk</u> can tell you the location of the luncheon.

    e. Ms. Gart wanted to improve the <u>company's</u> image.

2. Revise each of the following sentences to have pronoun/antecedent agreement.

    Example: Anyone who thinks that their car expenses will be small will probably be surprised.

    Revision: Anyone who thinks that <u>his or her</u> car expenses will be small will probably be surprised.

    a. Someone will have to sign their name to authorize delivery.

    b. The company has notified everyone about their responsibilities.

    c. No one of the administrative assistants plans to attend the seminar tomorrow.

    d. Each of the managers will be evaluated on their performance.

    e. The organization said that they will provide their members with emblems for their coats.

3. Revise each of the following sentences, inserting the appropriate interrogative or relative pronoun.

    Example: _____ did Mary hire to fill the position?

    Revision: <u>Whom</u> did Mary hire to fill the position?

    a. _____ presented the award to Mrs. Springer?

    b. To _____ are you sending the flowers?

    c. She is a person _____ you know well.

    d. Please give the package to _____ answers the door.

    e. Mrs. Carter, _____ house is on the corner, gives piano lessons.

4. List the appropriate form of the indefinite pronoun given in parentheses for each sentence.

    Example: I found _____ notebook. (somebody)

    Answer: I found <u>somebody's</u> notebook.

    a. We have not yet received _____ payment. (anybody)

    b. _____ car is usually parked in that zone. (someone)

    c. The manager appreciated _____ help. (everybody)

    d. _____ notes were left on the conference table. (somebody)

    e. The chairperson wanted to hear _____ ideas. (everyone)

5. In each of the following sentences, select the correct pronouns:

    a. Every student knows that (he or she, they) should attend class daily.

b. (We, us) supervisors will start our planning sessions tomorrow.
c. You can make (yourself, himself) proficient in grammar through dedicated practice.
d. They appointed (we, us) to work with the director of research.
e. You and (she, her) will represent our office at the seminar.
f. Was it (he, him) who made the sales presentation?
g. The firm will celebrate (its, it's) first anniversary next Thursday.
h. The person responsible for planning the dance will be (she, her).
i. They divided Patti's responsibilities between (her, she) and (me, I).
j. Each salesperson and each administrator set (his or her, their) goals for the coming year.

SECTION C

Verbs

Definition:
A **verb** is a word that tells what a subject does.

To express a thought, every sentence requires both a subject and a verb. The **subject** is a noun or pronoun naming what is being discussed. The **verb** is a word that (1) indicates action performed or received by the subject (*action verb*) or (2) joins modifiers to the subject (*linking* or *state-of-being* verb).

> An administrative assistant *keyed* the report. (action)
> The report *is* lengthy. (state of being)

Only verbs can show the timing of an action by changes in their spelling. Forms that show the timing of an action are called **tense forms**. The basic tense forms are present and past.

Present Tense	Past Tense
remember(s)	remembered
think(s)	thought
compute(s)	computed

become(s)   became
know(s)   knew

(Note: The *s* in the parentheses is used only with third-person singular subjects; e.g., That firm advertise*s* extensively.)

Main verbs and helping verbs

A sentence with a one-word verb is possible only in present and past tense.

Mrs. Adboul *takes* food to the needy.
Mr. Spieker *tore* his shirt on the nail.

In all other situations, a *verb phrase*—two or more verbs working together—is required. The last verb in a verb phrase is the **main verb**. The main verb conveys the key idea of the phrase. One or more helping verbs complete a verb phrase. The **helping verbs** often indicate the timing of the action. Some frequently used helping verbs are *has, have, do, did, can, must, will, would, should, is, was, were.*

	Helping Verb(s)	Main Verb	
The officers	have	finalized	their plans.
Mrs. Allen	will	write	the story.
The treasurer	is	collecting	the membership dues.

5.   Ms. Martinez can proofread and revise the bylaws.
6.   Many customers would have attended such a show.

ONE-FORM HELPING VERBS

Ten special helping verbs are unlike other helping verbs. These helping verbs have only one form and are always the first verb in any verb phrase. The ten special helping verbs include the following:

can   may   must   shall   will
could   might   ought   should   would

One-form helping verbs convey such meanings as ability, permission, possibility, obligation, and intention. *Shall* expresses simple future in first person, obligation in second and third persons. *Will* expresses determination in first person, simple future in second and third persons. (See page 28 for future tense information.)

I *shall* attend.
All applicants *must* appear.
Each employee *may* join.
Several clerks *should* have attended.
Mr. Hitako *will* be studying.
Mrs. Fouser *would* have been invited.

CHECK YOUR UNDERSTANDING 14

List the verbs in the following sentences under the headings "Verb Phrase", "Main Verb", and "One-Form Helping Verbs":

1.   The forms will have been distributed before August 10.
2.   All apprentices should be instructed about their duties.
3.   Several officials must approve such an action.
4.   I ought to confer with Miss Jasper about the program.
5.   Many athletes would have participated in the contests.

CLASSES OF VERBS

The classes of verbs are transitive, intransitive, and linking verbs. These classifications refer to main verbs only.

Transitive Verbs

Transitive verbs are action verbs followed by a noun or a pronoun that indicates what or who is affected by the action expressed by the verb.

	Transitive Verb	Noun or Pronoun
The child	closed	the door.
The architects	requested	them.
The student	gave	an entertaining report.

Intransitive Verbs

Intransitive verbs are not action verbs. Therefore, no additional nouns or pronouns are needed to receive action. However, modifiers often follow an intransitive verb.

	Intransitive Verb	Optional Modifiers
Seth	walked.	
Mandy	walked.	(quickly)
Several people	laughed.	(loudly)

Linking Verbs

Linking verbs join two nouns that refer to the same thing. Linking verbs can also join an adjective to a subject. (See Section D for information about adjectives.)

The most common linking verbs are forms of *to be—am, is, are, was, were*—and verb phrases ending in *been, be, being*. Other verbs commonly used as linking verbs are *smell, sound, taste, feel, look, seem, appear, become,* and *remain*.

	Linking Verb	Noun or Adjective
Mr. West	is	the manager.
The chairperson	was	Joan Keller.
The managers	are	supportive.
The roast	smells	delicious.
They	seem	happy.

CHECK YOUR UNDERSTANDING 15

List the verbs in the following sentences under the headings "Transitive Verbs," "Intransitive Verbs," and "Linking Verbs."

1. The community gave a contribution to the library.
2. They are students at the new high school.
3. After the rodeo, the people hurried out of the stands.
4. The study of the economy as a whole is macroeconomics.

5. Anna appeared calm.
6. We anticipate an increase in sales this year.
7. The consultants flew to Phoenix for a meeting with the company officers.
8. Mr. Adler remembered his appointment at the last minute.

PRINCIPAL PARTS OF VERBS

Verbs have three *principal parts*:

1. The *present tense*, (e.g., They *walk*, We *walk*)
2. The *past tense*, used without helping verbs (e.g., He *walked*)
3. The *past participle*, used *with* one or more helping verbs (e.g., *He has walked*)

Regular Verbs

To form the past tense and past participle of most regular verbs, add *-d* or *-ed* to the present tense. If a verb ends in *-y* preceded by a consonant, change the *y* to *i*, and add *-ed*. The past tense and past participle of regular verbs have the same spelling.

Present Tense	Past Tense	Past Participle
need	needed	needed
ship	shipped	shipped
present	presented	presented

Irregular Verbs

Irregular verbs change the spelling of their present tense to form the past tense and past participle. They may also add a *-t*, *-d*, *-ed*, or *-n* ending. The past tense and past participle of irregular verbs are sometimes different as shown in the commonly used irregular verbs in Table C-1 on pages 24-25.

CHECK YOUR UNDERSTANDING 16

Write the past tense and past participle of each of these verbs.

bring	lead	buy	lend
ring	teach	beat	throw
give	lie	swing	lay

TABLE C-1   COMMONLY USED IRREGULAR VERBS

Base Form	Past Tense	Past Participle	Base Form	Past Tense	Past Participle
arise	arose	arisen	hide	hid	hidden
be (am/are/is)	was/were	been	hit	hit	hit
bear	bore	borne/born	hold	held	held
become	became	become	hurt	hurt	hurt
begin	began	begun	keep	kept	kept
bend	bent	bent	know	knew	known
bid	bid	bid	lay	laid	laid
bind	bound	bound	lead	led	led
bite	bit	bitten/bit	leave	left	left
bleed	bled	bled	lend	lent	lent
blow	blew	blown	let	let	let
break	broke	broken	lie (recline)	lay	lain
bring	brought	brought	lose	lost	lost
broadcast	broadcast	broadcast	make	made	made
build	built	built	mean	meant	meant
burst	burst	burst	meet	met	met
buy	bought	bought	pay	paid	paid
choose	chose	chosen	put	put	put
come	came	come	quit	quit	quit
cost	cost	cost	read	read	read
cut	cut	cut	rid	rid	rid
deal	dealt	dealt	ride	rode	ridden
dig	dug	dug	ring	rang	rung
do	did	done	rise	rose	risen
draw	drew	drawn	run	ran	run
drink	drank	drunk	say	said	said
drive	drove	driven	see	saw	seen
eat	ate	eaten	seek	sought	sought
fall	fell	fallen	sell	sold	sold
feed	fed	fed	send	sent	sent
feel	felt	felt	set	set	set
find	found	found	shake	shook	shaken
flee	fled	fled	shine	shone	shone
forget	forgot	forgotten	shoot	shot	shot
freeze	froze	frozen	shrink	shrank	shrunk
give	gave	given	shut	shut	shut
go	went	gone	sing	sang	sung
grind	ground	ground	sink	sank	sunk
hang (suspend)	hung	hung	sit	sat	sat
have	had	had	sleep	slept	slept
hear	heard	heard	slit	slit	slit

Base Form	Past Tense	Past Participle	Base Form	Past Tense	Past Participle
speak	spoke	spoken	teach	taught	taught
speed	sped	sped	tear	tore	torn
spin	spun	spun	tell	told	told
split	split	split	think	thought	thought
spread	spread	spread	throw	threw	thrown
stand	stood	stood	understand	understood	understood
steal	stole	stolen	wear	wore	worn
stick	stuck	stuck	weave	wove	woven
sting	stung	stung	weep	wept	wept
strike	struck	struck	win	won	won
string	strung	strung	wind	wound	wound
swear	swore	sworn	wring	wrung	wrung
sweep	swept	swept	write	wrote	written
swim	swam	swum			

TABLE C-1   CONTINUED

SUBJECT-VERB AGREEMENT

A verb must agree with its subject in person and in number. Follow these rules for subject-verb agreement.

1.   A singular subject requires a singular verb. A singular verb ends with an *s* in the present tense, third person, singular.

> The production manager prepares schedules.
> She calculates the discounts carefully.
> This marketing strategy works very well.

2.   A plural subject requires a plural verb. A plural verb does not end in *s*.

> Our production managers prepare those schedules.
> They calculate the discounts carefully.
> These marketing strategies work very well.

AGREEMENT OF SUBJECT AND *BE*

Be is the only verb that has three different forms in the present tense: *am* and *is* (singular) and *are* (plural). (Note: *Are* is always used when *you* is the subject.)

> I *am* a football fan.
> You *are* correct about the date.
> She *is* excited about her European tour.

They *are* interested in safety.
Sue's aunt *is* a good interior decorator.

Be is also the only verb that has two different forms in the past tense: *was* (singular) and *were* (plural). (Note: *Were* is always used when *you* is the subject.)

I *was* early for the first class.
You *were* not at Wednesday's meeting.
He *was* a department supervisor.
They *were* extremely courteous to us.

CHECK YOUR UNDERSTANDING 17

Revise the following sentences to correct any subject-verb agreement errors:

1. We seen that movie last week.
2. Five bags of money was delivered by the security firm.
3. Several executives exercises at the Madison Health Club.
4. He don't have enough money to buy the car.
5. The manuals is needed by the company next Friday.

AGREEMENT WITH THIRD-PERSON SUBJECTS

The general rule is that singular subjects take singular verbs and plural subjects take plural verbs. With third-person subjects, interpret this rule as follows:

1. *Compound subjects* require plural verbs. A **compound subject** is two or more subjects joined by *and*.

   Miss Resnik and Mrs. Hodges are best friends.
   The manager and the secretary have a meeting to attend.
   The names and addresses were sent to the alumni office.

2. Compound subjects modified by *each* or *every* require singular verbs.

   Every man and woman in the firm is a loyal employee.
   Each policy manual and book was carefully packed.
   Every shirt and every tie is color coordinated.

3. Compound subjects joined by *or* or *nor* require a singular verb if the part of the subject nearer the verb is singular. They require a plural verb if the part of the subject nearer the verb is plural.

   The dogs or the cat was placed in the kennel.
   The cat or the dogs were fed early.

Neither low grades nor poor attendance makes a favorable impression on prospective employees.

4. Subjects that are plural in form but singular in meaning require singular verbs.

    The news brings other parts of the world closer to home.
    Economics is an interesting topic.
    Parrish & Company has a new president.
    Twenty dollars was the price of the dinner.
    My friend and confidant (one person) is a leader in the business community.

5. Subjects that are singular in form but plural in meaning are often followed by plural verbs. (Note: Some firms prefer to use singular verbs in this situation.) When the word *number* is used as the subject, use a plural verb if *number* is preceded by *a*; use a singular verb if *number* is preceded by *the*.

    A number of new houses are being built in the area.
    Some of the cars were moved to another lot.
    A great variety of styles are displayed.

6. Collective nouns as subjects may be used with singular or plural verbs. If you wish to emphasize the group as a unit, use a singular verb. If you wish to emphasize that individuals are acting separately, use a plural verb.

    The faculty meets once a month.
    The committee were assigned various responsibilities.

CHECK YOUR UNDERSTANDING 18

Rewrite the following sentences, and correct all errors in subject-verb agreement:

1. The lawyer and his client has reviewed the contract.
2. Each chair, desk, and computer were labeled.
3. Many letters has been sent to my office.
4. The flight attendants or the pilot are going to welcome the passengers.
5. Every man and woman in the group have volunteered to answer telephones at the telethon.
6. Neither the teachers nor the principal like the policy.
7. A number of managers is planning to work overtime next week.

TENSES

English has six tenses. **Present tense** tells what is happening now. **Past tense** tells what has already happened. **Future tense** tells what will happen.

Present perfect tense indicates an action begun in the past and completed in the present. **Past perfect tense** indicates an action begun in the past and completed in the past. **Future perfect tense** indicates an action begun in the past which will be completed in the future.

Present and past tenses do not require helping verbs. Other tenses do require helping verbs.

Present Tense	**Present Perfect Tense**
He sells the house.	He has sold the house.
Past Tense	**Past Perfect Tense**
He sold the house.	He had sold the house.
Future Tense	**Future Perfect Tense**
He will sell the house.	He will have sold the house.

CHECK YOUR UNDERSTANDING 19

Write the tense of the verbs in the following sentences:

1. Mr. Speer won the award for selling the most cars.
2. Miss Ramsey will work in the finance department.
3. Stephen has broken that chair twice.
4. They will have settled the problem by May 15.
5. The rancher had sold the cattle earlier in the year.
6. Everyone lends a hand to get the work done.

ACTIVE/PASSIVE VOICE

If the subject of the verb performs the action indicated by the verb, the verb is in **active voice**.

Shirley *read* eight books last month.
Mr. Conley *has dictated* the memo.
The candidate *will visit* four states in the next month.

If the subject receives the action indicated by the verb, the verb is in **passive voice**. Passive voice requires a form of *be* as a helping verb. In passive voice, the performer of the action may be omitted or indicated through a *by* phrase.

The fruit *was eaten* by the girls.
The weeds *have been sprayed*.
The furniture *will be moved* by the owners.

CHECK YOUR UNDERSTANDING 20

Without changing verb tense, revise the following sentences, making each verb active voice:

1. The blue sofa was selected by Mrs. Kingsley.
2. Many pictures have been hung by the decorator.
3. Before the convention, the minutes will have been mailed by the secretary.
4. The message had been sent by Mr. Hite.
5. The numbers will be analyzed by the auditor.

Without changing verb tense, revise the following sentences, making each verb passive voice:

1. That store kept the cost of merchandise as low as possible.
2. Mr. Hurt wrote the instructions for the contest yesterday.
3. The manager approved the plans.
4. Miss Kinney explained the benefits of the course.
5. By Thursday, Mr. Jacobs will have completed the painting.

INDICATIVE/SUBJUNCTIVE MOOD

Sentences that make statements of fact have verbs in the **indicative mood**. Most verbs in business messages are in indicative mood. All verbs discussed so far in this section have been in indicative mood.

In the **subjunctive mood**, verbs have unusual forms. The following situations require the subjunctive mood:

1. In expressions of conditions contrary to reality

    If I *were* you, I would work to build self-confidence.
    If Mr. Jackson *were* entered, he would win the race.
    If the manual *were* here, we could revise it to be clearer.

2. In formula-like expressions of hope

    Long *live* the free enterprise.

3. After verbs reporting commands, requests, and desires

    Mr. Marques asked that the blue car *be* moved.
    The director requested that Miss Kile *respond* at once.
    Mrs. Cape suggested that he *visit* the plant on Tuesday.

Revise the following sentences to use subjunctive mood appropriately:

1. The manager asked that Larry is relocated.
2. If Helen was at the meeting, she would help us with parliamentary procedure.
3. Miss Kim requested that the meeting begins immediately.
4. The group asked that special consideration is given to Mrs. Mathis.
5. If I was rich, I would travel around the world.

VERBALS

Verbals are verb forms that can be used as nouns (*infinitives* and *gerunds*) or as adjectives (*past participles* and *present participles*).

Verbals Used as Nouns

Infinitives are the present tense of the verb preceded by the word *to*.

> *To read* rapidly takes practice.
> Mrs. Zacha wants *to join* several organizations.
> Mr. Wommack likes *to go* to the baseball game.
> *To win* the game requires teamwork.
> My goal is *to see* the company grow.

Gerunds are the present tense of the verb plus the ending *-ing*.

> *Sailing* requires skill and strength.
> Our marketing manager enjoys *swimming* each morning.
> For *making* presentations, he brought a flip chart.
> *Eating* correctly promotes good health.

Use a possessive case noun or pronoun *before* a gerund.

> I appreciate *your* taking the children to the movie.
> The *dog's* barking kept me awake all night.
> *Shirley's* winning the sales contest was a pleasant surprise.

Verbals Used as Adjectives

Past participles are the third principal part of verbs.

> *Forgotten* items sometimes become valuable antiques.
> The police found the *stolen* car.
> The manager apologized for the *delayed* order.

Present participles are the present tense of the verb plus the ending *-ing*. Present participles and gerunds are identical in spelling but different in use.

> *Standing* on the corner, the man waved to his neighbor who drove by.
> The attorney *handling* your case took the files with him.
> Mrs. Ramsey, *understanding* her daughter's situation, wrote a sensitive note.

CHECK YOUR UNDERSTANDING 22

Rewrite the following sentences, and insert the verb in parentheses, using the appropriate verbal. Be prepared to explain why you used each verbal.

1. Jenny was injured when she fell off the _____ swing. (broke)
2. The song _____ by Elaine was written by an American composer. (sing)
3. Someone needs _____ a new policy manual soon. (write)
4. _____ a book every month is a real challenge. (read)
5. _____ carefully each night will improve your grades. (study)
6. Our staff is expected _____ extra hours next week. (work)
7. _____ two miles each day is excellent exercise. (walk)
8. I enjoy _____ you with your homework. (help)

EDITING APPLICATIONS

1. Identify the helping verb and the main verb in each of the following sentences.

   Example: The contractor has begun to build many new homes in our neighborhood.
   Answer: helping verb—has; main verb—begun

   a. My uncle did keep his antique car.
   b. The workers have laid all the bricks for the sidewalk.
   c. Because of the low temperature, most plants were frozen last night.
   d. Our team will win the tennis tournament.
   e. To obtain the discount, you must return the enclosed form.

2. Write the verbs in the following sentences under the headings "Transitive Verbs," "Intransitive Verbs," and "Linking Verbs."

   Example: That nurse is a compassionate person.
   Answer: linking verb—is

   a.   The choir sang loudly during the concert.
   b.   As people age, their bones become fragile.
   c.   The child had drunk two glasses of milk by noon.
   d.   Susan sat on the sofa for several minutes.
   e.   All the administrative assistants were happy about the raise.

3. Compose a sentence using the past participle of each of the following verbs.

   Example: throw
   Answer: The ball *was thrown* at the target.

   a.   pull
   b.   lie
   c.   see
   d.   lay
   e.   ring

4. In the following sentences, identify the complete verbs and the verb tenses.

   Example: The dog lies in the water in hot weather.
   Answer: verb—lies; tense—present

   a.   Al advertised his restaurant in the newspaper.
   b.   Alice had written to the human resources director about the position.
   c.   The letter has lain on her desk for several days.
   d.   Editing files on the computer is easy.
   e.   We shall have planned the entire convention by tonight.
   f.   I lay the books next to the record sheets every evening.
   g.   Define spreadsheets and list ways to use them.
   h.   Graphics were used to show the results of the survey.
   i.   Their curriculum has been identified as one of the most outstanding in the state.
   j.   The phone rang three times before anyone answered.

5. Revise the sentences on page 33, changing the verbs in passive voice to active voice. Make necessary changes in phrasing, but do not change the tense of the verbs.

   Example: The story was told by Douglas.
   Revision: Douglas told the story.

   a. The convention program has been planned by a committee.
   b. Arrangements have been made for the buffet by Mr. Jabara.
   c. The order for tennis shoes was mailed by Coach Davis.
   d. The furniture had been polished carefully by Marian.
   e. The grant proposal was revised by the department chairperson.

6. Correct all errors in subject-verb agreement or in mood.

   Example: Fifty dollars are expensive for a book.
   Revision: Fifty dollars is expensive for a book.

   a. Their applications is due by July 1.
   b. Mr. Katlin requested that the due date for his report is extended.
   c. It don't look like it will rain today.
   d. Neither of the employees were interested in assuming more responsibilities.
   e. The vice president and the general manager is extremely dependable and cooperative.
   f. A number of persons is planning to drive to the lake.
   g. The staff have given its complete support.
   h. Either Martha or her sisters is enrolled in that computer class.
   i. Half of the messages is for the sales representative.
   j. He said that the proceeds from the sales is easy to calculate.

SECTION D

Adjectives

Definition:
An **adjective** is a word that modifies a noun or a pronoun.

LIMITING AND DESCRIPTIVE ADJECTIVES

The two kinds of adjectives are limiting adjectives and descriptive adjectives.

Limiting adjectives indicate which (e.g., *this, a, those*) or how many (e.g., *all, several, five*) things are being referred to in a sentence. **Descriptive adjectives** assign characteristics (e.g., *courteous, large,* *cooperative, helpful*) to whatever is named by the modified noun or pronoun.

Limiting Adjective	Descriptive Adjective	Modified Noun
an	intelligent	person
a	sincere	thought
the	red	dress
several	dependable	employees
every	capable	manager
one	good	reason
those	American	flags
four	positive	responses
numerous	good	ideas

A and *an* are different forms of the same word. Use *a* when the next word begins with the sound of a consonant. Use *an* when the next word begins with the sound of a vowel.

A before Consonant Sound	An before Vowel Sound
*a f*irm	*an o*ccasion
*a c*olleague	*an a*pple
*a u*nit (Unit begins with the consonant sound *y*.)	*an h*eir (*H* is silent. Heir begins with a vowel sound.)

Possessive pronouns such as *my, your, his, her, its, our,* and *their* also function as limiting adjectives.

> *Your* dress is very attractive.
> Kathy will ride *her* horse in the parade.

Possessive nouns also function as limiting adjectives.

> The *girl's* notebook was on the desk.
> The committee *members'* answers surprised many people.

CHECK YOUR UNDERSTANDING 23

Rewrite the following sentences, and insert either a limiting adjective, a descriptive adjective, or a possessive pronoun or noun:

1. He entered _____ poster in three contests.
2. _____ applicant should be neatly dressed.
3. Miss Rodey served _____ customers during the noon hour.
4. The teacher made copies of _____ sales letter to show the class.

5. Most of the members were _____ about the changes.
6. Janey offered to have the meeting at _____ home.

ADJECTIVE ENDINGS

Many descriptive adjectives are formed by adding characteristic endings to other words. For example, you may form the adjective *inventive* by adding the ending *-ive* to the verb *invent*.

Below is a list of adjective-endings and examples of adjectives formed with those endings.

Adjective Ending	Source Word	Descriptive Adjective
able	return	returnable
al	addition	additional
ant	hesitate	hesitant
ary	compliment	complimentary
ate	consider	considerate
cal	economy	economical
ent	consist	consistent
ful	resource	resourceful
ial	industry	industrial
ible	sense	sensible
ish	fool	foolish
ive	compete	competitive
like	business	businesslike
ly	friend	friendly
ous	continue	continuous
y	worth	worthy

CHECK YOUR UNDERSTANDING 24

Write adjectives based on the following words:

finance	logic	fame
like	flex	supplement
persist	child	fool

PREDICATE ADJECTIVES

Predicate adjectives describe the subject and follow linking verbs. (See Section C for information on linking verbs.)

The carpenters were *careful* when they built that house.
That lady is *happy* about her trip to Mexico.
He appeared *calm* before he gave his presentation.
The casserole tastes *delicious*, and the cake looks *beautiful*.

CHECK YOUR UNDERSTANDING 25

List the predicate adjectives in the following sentences:

1. The fresh flowers smelled pretty.
2. Claudia was helpful in planning the project.
3. Mrs. Diaz was pleased when her supervisor gave her a raise.
4. I feel annoyed about having to work late tonight.
5. With practice, you can become proficient at painting quality seascapes.

DEGREES OF COMPARISON

Writers frequently make comparisons involving descriptive adjectives. Use special forms and phrases for adjectives in these comparisons. The three degrees of comparison are positive, comparative, and superlative.

Positive degree is the base form of the adjective. Use the positive degree (1) when introducing a comparison with *as* or *not as* (e.g., *strong*, *cooperative*) and (2) when no explicit comparison is involved.

> Her idea is *good*.
> Her idea is as *good* as Tammy's.
> Her idea is not as *good* as Amy's.

Use the **comparative degree** when a comparison involves one item that is superior (or inferior) to a second one or to any other item in the group (e.g., *stronger, more cooperative*).

One-syllable adjectives and many two-syllable adjectives add the ending *-er* to form the comparative degree. Other adjectives use the comparative helping word *more* (*less* in negative comparisons).

Comparative Degree (using *-er*-ending)	Comparative Degree (using *more* or *less*)
clearer	more satisfactory
faster	more pleasing
greater	more important
duller	more constructive
healthier	less efficient

Than usually follows the comparative degree of adjectives. After *than*, use such expressions as *anyone else* or *anything else* rather than *anyone* or *anything*. Also, use *any other* instead of *any* when something is individually compared in its own group.

Illogical	Logical
Mrs. Edmonds is more likable than anyone on the committee.	Mrs. Edmonds is more likable than *anyone else* on the committee.
Our tables are sturdier than any tables on the market.	Our tables are sturdier than *any other* tables on the market.

Use the **superlative degree** when one unit is the best (*worst* in negative comparisons) of all those considered (e.g., *strongest, most cooperative*).

Adjectives that use *-er* to form the comparative degree, use *-est* to form the superlative degree. Those that use *more* (*less* in negative comparisons) for the comparative degree use *most* (*least* in negative comparisons) for the superlative degree.

Superlative Degree (using *-est*-ending)	Superlative Degree (using *most* or *least*)
clearest	most satisfactory
fastest	most pleasing
greatest	most important
dullest	most constructive
healthiest	least efficient

Usually use the superlative degree in comparisons involving more than two items. However, you may use the superlative degree for emphasis even when no comparison is expressed.

Henry Smithson is a most interesting speaker.

IRREGULAR FORMS FOR DEGREES OF COMPARISON

Irregular adjectives are adjectives whose comparative and superlative degrees are not forms of the same word as their positive degree.

Positive Degree	Comparative Degree	Superlative Degree
bad	worse	worst
good	better	best

little	less	least
much	more	most
well (healthy)	better	best

CHECK YOUR UNDERSTANDING 26

For each of the following sentences, write the appropriate form for the adjective in parentheses:

1. On Saturday, Mrs. Wade prepared the (good) meal served this week.
2. Moore & Company has a (large) number of credit customers than its competitor.
3. Property taxes are the (high) of the five taxes we have to pay.
4. Mr. Campbell is as (happy) as I have ever seen him.
5. This insulation is (efficient) than the insulation we used last year.

ABSOLUTE ADJECTIVES

Adjectives like *unique, round, square, full, correct,* and *perfect* are used only in the positive degree. (They cannot be compared.) A thing is either unique (meaning *one of a kind*) or not unique, round or not round. Therefore, saying that something is "more unique" or "rounder" than something else is illogical.

COMPOUND ADJECTIVES

A **compound adjective** is two or more words used as a unit to describe a noun or pronoun.

soft-spoken man	on-the-job training
interest-bearing note	an eight-year-old girl
good-natured person	a true-false test

1. Hyphenate most compound adjectives when they precede the modified noun. Usually avoid hyphenating a compound adjective that follows the modified noun.

well-known speaker	The speaker is well known.
long-range goals	The editor's goals were long range.

2. Hyphenate the compound adjective that is composed of a number and a noun.

a 30-mile trip	a three-year contract
a 75-cent computer fee	a two-week vacation

3.   Some compound nouns are used as compound adjectives and are not hyphenated.

>   real estate office
>   income tax payment
>   high school student

CHECK YOUR UNDERSTANDING 27

Revise the following sentences, correcting the adjective forms:

1.   The reporter's article was most unique.
2.   The executive will leave Monday for a three week vacation.
3.   Since we have an up to date address list, we can send the announcements immediately.
4.   She received an award for having the most perfect essay.
5.   As a real-estate agent, Mandy earns an excellent income.

EDITING APPLICATIONS

1.   In the following sentences, list the limiting adjectives and descriptive adjectives under the headings "Limiting Adjectives" and "Descriptive Adjectives".

   Example: A quiet story should help the child go to sleep.
   Answer: limiting adjectives—a, the
                 descriptive adjective—quiet

   a.   A strong wind makes a good source of power.
   b.   The students submitted 20 reports for the English teacher to read.
   c.   He conducted the meeting in a businesslike manner.
   d.   Her attitude about the move is cooperative and realistic.
   e.   An automobile insurance policy is essential.
   f.   She learned how to create a data base file, to print form letters, and to merge two programs.
   g.   That class is designed to instill a competitive spirit in future entrepreneurs.
   h.   The company contributed four complimentary tickets.

2.   Identify the degree of comparison in each of the following sentences.

   Example: Stuart studies harder than any other boy in the class.
   Answer: comparative degree

   a.   This computer is the most versatile computer in the exhibit.
   b.   Mr. Vink is more qualified than any other accountant in the office.

    c. The test was easy because I studied last night.
    d. Abilene is larger than any other city in the area.
    e. She is the eldest of five children.
    f. This coat is less expensive than any other coat in the store.
    g. Of the two cities, Atlanta is closer.
    h. Tad gave an excellent presentation last week.
    i. The stock car race was the most exciting event of the day.
    j. These electric blankets are less expensive than those.

3. List the adjectives in the following sentences.

    Example: Your new book is interesting and beneficial.
    Answer: adjectives—your, new, interesting, beneficial

    a. His busy teacher will grade the term papers by Friday.
    b. The ballet dancer was happy that she was selected to perform in their last production of the year.
    c. Before Janet can use the new computer, she must take ten lessons in your department.
    d. Be sure to send an up-to-date list to the new supervisor.
    e. He will travel 4,200 miles on his three-week trip to four European countries.

4. Choose the correct adjective from those given in parentheses.

    Example: Evelyn works (harder, hardest) than any other gymnast.
    Answer: harder

    a. Of all the children in the room, Jim is the (younger, youngest).
    b. Many of the science projects were interesting, but Anthony's was (unique, most unique).
    c. When you use the computer keyboard, use the (lighter, lightest) touch possible.
    d. Of all the estimates we received, yours is the (less expensive, least expensive).
    e. Both watches are well made, but this one is (better, best).

5. Revise the following sentences, correcting all adjective errors.

    Example: In the duet, Shawn sang loudest.
    Revision: In the duet, Shawn sang louder.

    a. She wrote an detailed report.
    b. Even though she is the newest committee member, she is more conscientious than any committee member.
    c. Of the two cities, is Dallas or Denver farthest from Las Vegas?
    d. This is a most perfect circle.
    e. Please send me up to the minute information about stock options.

f. Which sister is the oldest, Mary or Judith?
g. The more interesting speaker of all was the business executive.
h. That is the worse example of neatness I have ever seen.
i. This house is larger than any house on the block.
j. Jack Monroe won the position in a city wide election.

SECTION E

Adverbs

Definition:
An **adverb** is a word which modifies a verb, an adjective, or another adverb.

KINDS OF ADVERBS

The four main kinds of adverbs are adverbs of time, place, manner, and degree. Adverbs of time answer the questions *when* and *how often*.
Common adverbs of time include the following:

after	immediately	presently
afterwards	instantly	rarely
before	late	seldom
beforehand	monthly	simultaneously
early	now	soon
eventually	often	then
frequently	once, twice, etc.	thereafter

She has used that computer program *often*.
Mr. Lovett *immediately* sent a contribution.
Many of the executives worked *late*.
The consultant reports *monthly* to the Dallas office.

Adverbs of place or direction answer the question *where*. Common adverbs of place or direction include the following:

across	in	outside	through
by	inside	over	under

down	near	past	up
here	out	there	upstairs

As soon as Mavis came home, she went *upstairs* to read.
The children played *outside* for two hours.
We left the car *there* while we went to the movies.
To reach the lake, we drove *north* on Interstate 25.

Adverbs of manner answer the question *how* and are usually formed by adding -*ly* to a descriptive adjective. Examples of adverbs of manner include the following:

busily	happily	profitably	separately
casually	highly	quietly	sincerely
comfortably	lazily	randomly	slowly
enthusiastically	patiently	rapidly	well

Joseph responded to the question *enthusiastically*.
John *sincerely* believed that he could repair the car in two hours.
Lynda *casually* mentioned that she planned to fly to Rapid City on Friday.

Adverbs of degree and extent answer such questions as *how much* and *to what extent*. Examples of adverbs of degree and extent include the following:

completely	greatly	not
entirely	however (e.g.,	partly
exceedingly	*however* costly)	too (meaning
extensively	little	excessively)
extraordinarily	much	thoroughly
fully	nearly	very

The fire damaged the building *extensively*.
The guests *thoroughly* enjoyed the dinner.
The sofa was *too* large for the available wall space.

CHECK YOUR UNDERSTANDING 28

Write an appropriate adverb to complete each of the following sentences. Use a different adverb in each sentence.

1. Lawson & Lawson _____ employs 30 attorneys.
2. Each of us should drive _____ in a school zone.
3. Mrs. Dunn explained the math problem _____ .

4.   Set the bowl of potatoes _____ .
5.   Staci _____ ignored her mother's warning about driving fast.

DEGREES OF COMPARISON

Like adjectives, you may use adverbs in comparisons. Accordingly, such adverbs have forms for positive, comparative, and superlative degrees. Use the endings *-er* and *-est* and the helping words *more* and *most* (*less* and *least* in negative comparisons) with adverbs just as you do with adjectives. (See Section D.)

Positive	Comparative	Superlative
They traveled *far*.	They traveled *farther*.	They traveled *farthest*.
We drove *fast*.	We drove *faster*.	We drove *fastest*.
He did *little*.	He did *less*.	He did the *least*.
Alice attends *frequently*.	Alice attends *more frequently*.	Alice attends *most frequently*.

The patterns of phrasing with adverbs in positive, comparative, and superlative degrees are similar to those used with adjectives. (See Section D.)

Mr. Spiney arrives *early*.
Mr. Spiney arrives *as early as* Mr. Harwell.
Mr. Spiney arrives *earlier* than any other partner.
Mr. Spiney arrives *earliest* of all the partners.

CHECK YOUR UNDERSTANDING 29

From those given in parentheses, select the appropriate degree of the adverb to complete the following sentences:

1.   The senior sponsor described the planned trip (enthusiastically) than any other sponsor.
2.   My parents arrived (early) than Kelli's parents.
3.   Of all the persons in the room, Katherine answered the questions (well).
4.   Anita travels (frequently) than most people do.
5.   Of the three applicants, Miss Penney was dressed (appropriately).

PLACEMENT OF ADVERBS

Place adverbs that modify adjectives and adverbs immediately before the term they modify.

completely honest	*too* extensive
seldom angry	*thoroughly* comfortable
extremely courteously	*very* competently

You may place adverbs that modify verbs in various positions. At the beginning or end of a sentence, they receive special attention.

Patiently, Ms. Spees waited for the results.
The contestant *nervously* answered the questions.
The initiates *confidently* repeated the pledge.

Place the adverbs *only, not, merely*, and the adverbial phrase *at least* immediately before the term they modify.

Careless Placement	Effective Placement
This dress only costs $42.	This dress costs only $42.
By this morning, we had only received 12 responses.	By this morning, we had received only 12 responses.
Every person did not resign.	Not every person resigned.
Joanie at least sang four songs.	Joanie sang at least four songs.

CHECK YOUR UNDERSTANDING 30

Rewrite the following sentences, and insert at the most appropriate point the adverb given in parentheses:

1. The members at the convention elected three officers. (only; i.e., no more than three)
2. The team won three games last year. (eventually)
3. Every person paid the registration fee. (not)
4. We are in need of additional staff members. (critically)
5. Sharon mentioned the ticket cost. (merely; i.e., no more than mentioned)

VERB-ADVERB COMBINATIONS

Idioms are phrases, in this case verbs and adverbs, that have been used together so frequently they have special meanings.

The secretary *looked up* the word she didn't know how to spell.
Miss Jenson, the accountant, *sent out* his 250-page report.

The soldier *carried out* his superiors' orders.
The campaign manager *spoke out* in the candidate's defense.
Ms. Bobacek *ran into* Mr. Krause in the grocery store.

CHECK YOUR UNDERSTANDING 31

Write an appropriate adverb to complete a verb-adverb combination in each of the following sentences:

1. Maxine tried _____ the bicycle exerciser in the store.
2. Mr. Landers held _____ the payment for a week.
3. The lawyer said that he would look _____ the contract more thoroughly.
4. Vera ran _____ Miss Walters at the meeting.
5. Vice President Walker carried _____ the plans.

VALUE OF ADVERBS

Every sentence must have a subject (noun or pronoun) and a verb. In contrast, a sentence can be a sentence without adverbs. However, adverbs often convey essential information. In a letter of recommendation, the following sentences *with* adverbs would help secure an interview for an applicant. Those sentences without adverbs would not be effective.

Ineffective	Effective
Miss Roland speaks.	Miss Roland speaks intelligently and honestly.
Miss Norris answers the phone.	Miss Norris answers the phone courteously and professionally.
Mr. Adams works.	Mr. Adams works cooperatively and enthusiastically.

CHECK YOUR UNDERSTANDING 32

Write a different adverb to complete each of the following sentences:

1. The doctor listens to his patients _____ .
2. To improve his health, Mr. Eden eats _____ .
3. Sherry came to the firm _____ recommended.

4. My teacher grades papers _____ .
5. President Muncie will _____ receive the award.

EDITING APPLICATIONS

1. List each adverb in the following sentences under one of the following headings: "Time," "Place," "Manner," or "Degree."

   Example: Dave went outside after he finished unpacking.
   Answer: place—outside

   a. Jason carefully completed the painting for the art exhibit.
   b. When the chairperson asked for volunteers for the refreshment committee, B. J. raised his hand immediately.
   c. Mrs. Petrick has completely recovered from her surgery.
   d. Kisha went there to register for a Spanish course.
   e. Charlene thoroughly enjoyed the concert last night.

2. List the adverbs in the following sentences.

   Example: Mr. Reese convincingly presented his views to the staff.
   Answer: convincingly

   a. She changed her plans considerably because of the very heavy rain.
   b. Jeffrey and Marlowe proceeded cautiously along the treacherous trail.
   c. Bill's mother was somewhat relieved to find him already there.
   d. The election was extremely close, so the election committee recounted the votes carefully.
   e. Mr. Jackson went inside and promptly greeted all his friends and relatives.

3. For each sentence, list the appropriate degree of comparison for the adverb in parentheses.

   Example: Miss Hobby made sales _____ than any other representative in the region. (often)
   Answer: *more often*

   a. Miss Saks greets visitors _____ than Mr. Wilcox does. (graciously)
   b. Miss Linx designed the advertisement that increased sales _____ of all. (much)
   c. The new copier performs _____ than the old one. (good)

     d. Mr. Hurd arrived for the meeting _____ than anyone else. (early)

     e. The accounting department performs its duties _____ than any other department. (reliably)

4. Revise the following sentences, correcting any adverb-related errors.

Example: Those shoes only cost $39.
Revision: Those shoes cost <u>only</u> $39.

     a. Every employee did not leave early.
     b. Miss Wilson only paid $25 for that lamp.
     c. You can accomplish your goals easy.
     d. Betty decided to cancel the garage sale because she did not feel good.
     e. Send the order as quick as possible.

SECTION F

Prepositions

Definition:
A **preposition** is a word that joins a noun or a pronoun to some other part of the sentence.

COMMONLY USED PREPOSITIONS

Most prepositions are single words. Prepositions which consist of more than one word are called **phrasal prepositions**.

about	because of	by	for
above	before	by means of	from
across	behind	by reason of	in
after	below	by virtue of	in addition to
against	beneath	by virtue of	in front of
along	beside	concerning	in lieu of
among	between	despite	in place of
around	beyond	down	in spite of
at	but *(except)*	during	instead of
		except	

into	on account of	throughout	unto
like	on behalf of	till	up
near	out	to	upon
next	over	toward	with
of	past	under	within
off	since	underneath	without
on	through	until	

PREPOSITIONAL PHRASES

A preposition and the noun or pronoun it joins to another part of the sentence are called a **prepositional phrase**. The noun or pronoun that follows the preposition is the *object of the preposition*. Every prepositional phrase must have *both* a preposition and an object, and the object may have modifiers. In the following prepositional phrases, the prepositions are underlined; the nouns as objects are italicized.

> with the *banker*
> from the brick *house*
> on the *desk*
> in front of the tall *building*
> before the *meeting*
> through the long *tunnel*

The object of a preposition may be a pronoun as well as a noun. A personal pronoun used as the object of a preposition *must* be in the objective case (*me, you, her, him, us, them*).

In the following prepositional phrases, the prepositions are underlined, and the pronouns used as objects are capitalized:

> to HIM
> between YOU and ME
> for US and THEM
> without YOU and HER
> except US
> for ME

CHECK YOUR UNDERSTANDING 33

For each of the following prepositional phrases, list the appropriate form of the pronoun:

1. from _____ (I)
2. with _____ and _____ (he and she)
3. above _____ (they)
4. between _____ and _____ (you and I)

5. behind _____ (we)
6. except _____ (I)
7. without _____ and _____ (he and I)
8. toward _____ (they)
9. to _____ and _____ (she and I)
10. in spite of _____ (they)

USES OF PREPOSITIONAL PHRASES

Prepositional phrases can be joined to a subject, verb, object, or modifier. Prepositional phrases become modifiers of the word to which they are joined. When prepositional phrases modify a noun or a pronoun, such phrases are used as adjectives and answer *which one* or *what kind* questions. When they modify a verb, adjective, or adverb, they are used as adverbs and answer questions, such as *how, when, where, why, how often, how much,* and *to what extent.*

Below are examples of prepositional phrases modifying various parts of speech. The prepositional phrases are printed in capital letters; the modified word is underlined.

The cost OF CLOTHES has increased.
Somebody FROM THE GROUP will go.
Mr. Elkins rode IN THE LIMOUSINE.
Pleased ABOUT THE PRICE, Ms. Langston signed the contract.
Fortunately FOR MS. EATON, a doctor was present.

PLACEMENT OF PREPOSITIONAL PHRASES

Prepositional phrases that modify a noun, pronoun, adjective, or adverb follow the part they modify. In contrast, prepositional phrases that modify a verb may precede or follow the verb or come between a helping verb and the main verb. Place such a prepositional phrase where you achieve the desired emphasis. A prepositional phrase will get the most attention at the beginning or end of a sentence.

At the convention, Mrs. Adams will introduce the speaker.
Mrs. Adams, at the convention, will introduce the speaker.
Mrs. Adams will, at the convention, introduce the speaker.
Mrs. Adams will introduce the speaker at the convention.

List appropriate prepositions to complete each sentence.

1. Chris enjoyed the demonstration _____ the latest office equipment.
2. The reputation _____ that firm has been built _____ high standards.
3. _____ you and me, I think the plan will be a huge success.
4. My children will be _____ me _____ the weekend celebration.
5. If you will wait _____ 1:00 p.m., we can have lunch together.

WORDS USED AS PREPOSITIONS AND ADVERBS

Some words commonly used as prepositions are also used as adverbs. Adverbs by themselves are modifiers. Prepositions by themselves are not modifiers. Prepositions are connecting words that link nouns and pronouns to other sentence parts. The resulting prepositional *phrases* are modifiers. In the following examples, the words used as adverbs are underlined:

> The girls drove around.
> They lagged behind.
> Boyd ran in.

In the following examples, the same words (*around*, *behind*, and *in*) are used as prepositions. The objects of the prepositions are underlined.

> The girls drove around the football stadium.
> They lagged behind the group.
> Boyd ran in the race yesterday.

List each adverb and prepositional phrase in the following sentences:

1. Everyone attended the special meeting except Jon.
2. The results of the election are being phoned in.
3. Dwayne waited inside while the two managers talked in the conference room.

4. Miss Morgan hurried off to meet Mrs. Dobbs at the airport.
5. According to the instructions, the representatives should meet outside by 5:00 p.m.

INAPPROPRIATE USE OF PREPOSITIONS

Omit unnecessary prepositions. Questions, often incorrectly contain unnecessary prepositions.

Wordy	**Concise**
Off of the table	Off the table
made out of wool	made of wool
looked out of the window	looked out the window
Where is he going to?	Where is he going?
Where is your car at?	Where is your car?
Where did she get off at?	Where did she get off?

CHECK YOUR UNDERSTANDING 36

Rewrite the following sentences, omitting unnecessary words:

1. Jana, where do you get off the bus at?
2. Where is Mr. Wells going to for lunch?
3. The paper weights are made out of marble and are heavy.
4. Mr. Quinn saw the car come off of the Moran Street exit.
5. What is that wrinkle-resistant material made out of?

EDITING APPLICATIONS

1. Revise the following sentences, replacing the proper nouns in the prepositional phrases with appropriate personal pronouns.

   Example: The proposal was supported by the contractor and *Vincent*.

   Revision: The proposal was supported by the contractor and him.

   a. The building lots were sold to neighbors and the Spencers.
   b. My cousins attended the performance with Miss Wang.

      c. We have received bids from two large corporations and Gerald Price.

      d. The new classes were divided between Ms. Collins and Mr. Price.

      e. A report from Mrs. Garth arrived yesterday.

2. Revise the following sentences by shifting the introductory prepositional phrase to another appropriate position to place greater emphasis on the subject of each sentence.

Example: *In a month*, you will be promoted.
Revision: You will be promoted in a month.

      a. Because of the revised policy, we will print new forms.
      b. Besides Margie and Randy, six people have indicated an interest.
      c. In addition to dependability, self-confidence, and persuasiveness, numerous qualities are necessary for effective leadership.
      d. Because of your initiative, the department has increased its sales volume tremendously.
      e. During the next six months, the training department will conduct five skill-development seminars.

3. Revise the following sentences, placing the prepositional phrases so that the meaning of each sentence is clearer.

Example: Mrs. Vinson sent to the treasurer her club dues.
Revision: Mrs. Vinson sent her club dues to the treasurer.

      a. Lucy made the decision for the committee about the mailing cost.
      b. We mailed our ideas to the travel agency for improving the tour.
      c. Mr. Darner submitted his request to his supervisor for a year's leave of absence.
      d. The price changes were enclosed for the art supplies in my last shipment.
      e. Miss Potter sold to a man from Orlando the couple's duplex.

4. Revise the following sentences, omitting unnecessary prepositions.

Example: Bev, where is the red folder *at*?
Revision: Bev, where is the red folder?

      a. Where did you park your car at?
      b. Where is the new office located at?
      c. Nancy got off of the tram at the department store.
      d. Please move that computer off of the desk.
      e. Mr. Stanton told us where he was going to, but he wasn't there when we called.

SECTION G

Conjunctions

Definition:
Conjunctions connect words, phrases (groups of words without a subject and verb), and clauses (groups of words with a subject and verb).

The three types of conjunctions are coordinating, correlative, and subordinating. In addition, linking adverbs are often used as conjunctions.

COORDINATING CONJUNCTIONS

Coordinating conjunctions join sentence elements of equal rank. They can join words, phrases, dependent clauses, and main clauses. The four most common coordinating conjunctions are *and, or, but, nor*.

> Cars *and* trucks . . . .
> In California *or* in New York . . . .
> If Mr. Roberts applies *and* if he wins . . . .
> We have the Trevino account, *but* we haven't seen the contract yet.
> They did not receive money, *nor* did they ask for any.

CHECK YOUR UNDERSTANDING 37

List an appropriate coordinating conjunction to complete each sentence.

1. Some of the doctors enjoyed the program, _____ others did not.
2. Mr. Ison _____ Mr. Jacobs will soon be presidents of their companies.
3. We can send the proposal to Miss Ellison _____ Mr. Johnson, whichever you prefer.

4. We have not received their recommendations, _____ have we asked for them.
5. When the assignments have been received _____ graded, we will discuss the next topic.

CORRELATIVE CONJUNCTIONS

Correlative conjunctions occur in pairs and join parts of equal rank. The most common correlative conjunctions are both . . . and, either . . . or, neither . . . nor, not only . . . but also, and whether . . . or.

> *Both* the computer *and* the printer . . . .
> *Either* pay the bill *or* return the furniture.
> Mr. Moss *neither* accepted *nor* rejected his suggestion.
> *Not only* beautiful *but also* intelligent . . . .
> I'm not sure *whether* to leave *or* to stay.

CHECK YOUR UNDERSTANDING 38

List an appropriate correlative conjunction to complete each of the following sentences:

1. Tom said that he will _____ watch television _____ go to a movie.
2. Mrs. Dreyer suggested that I _____ balance the checkbook _____ pay the bills.
3. _____ the certificates _____ the plaques were awarded last night at the dinner.
4. The firm is not sure _____ Carlton Stack _____ Ronnie Hamil wrote the report.

SUBORDINATING CONJUNCTIONS

Subordinating conjunctions join dependent clauses to main clauses. Common subordinating conjunctions include the following:

after	in order that	unless
although	provided	until
as	since	when
as if	so that	whenever
because	than	where
before	that	while
how	though	why
if		

Subordinating conjunctions introduce three types of dependent clauses—noun, adjective, and adverb clauses. In the following examples, the subordinating conjunctions are italicized and the dependent clauses are underlined:

Mrs. Durham said *that* <u>she would assist us</u>. (noun clause)
The idea *that* <u>you suggested</u> is excellent. (adjective clause)
Because <u>it snowed last week</u>, we postponed the trip. (adverb clause)

CHECK YOUR UNDERSTANDING 39

List a different subordinating conjunction to complete each sentence.

1. _____ you study supply and demand, you are learning an important economic concept.
2. The administrative assistant stated _____ her position is extremely rewarding.
3. It looks _____ we will get the contract.
4. She assured us _____ the payments were made on time.
5. The desks and chairs _____ you ordered on February 7 should arrive by March 25.
6. We will leave _____ we receive authorization.

LINKING ADVERBS

In addition to conjunctions, **linking adverbs** (sometimes called conjunctive adverbs) are useful as connectors. Common linking adverbs include the following:

accordingly	moreover
also	nevertheless
consequently	otherwise
further	still
furthermore	therefore
hence	thus
however	yet

Linking adverbs are often used to join the independent clauses of compound sentences. Linking adverbs may introduce the second clause or stand within it. Use a semicolon before the linking adverb and a comma after it when the linking adverb joins two independent clauses.

Costs are going up monthly; however, we will guarantee this price until June.

He said that he would help me build the fence; I doubt, however, that he will be available.

The main road is closed for two months; consequently, Dower & Company will not be open until June.

You may also use linking adverbs to draw attention to the connection between one sentence and a preceding sentence.

The luncheon will be held tomorrow. *However*, tickets are still available.

The toll road is faster than Interstate 35. *Moreover*, it is safer.

Many clients enjoyed the opportunity to visit our office. We will *therefore*, plan a larger reception next year.

CHECK YOUR UNDERSTANDING 40

List a different linking adverb to complete each of the following sentences:

1. Some employees like flexible work hours; _____ , others prefer regular hours.
2. Miss Austin has a speaking engagement in Omaha on May 4; _____ , she wants to arrive there on May 3.
3. The equipment has been purchased. _____ , it has not yet been delivered.
4. Personalized letters capture the receiver's attention; _____, all officers have developed their own letters.
5. Mrs. Cory attended the general sessions; _____ , she participated in some of the small-group meetings.

EDITING APPLICATIONS

1. List an appropriate coordinating conjunction to complete each sentence.

   a. George was told that he received a promotion, _____ the public announcement is yet to be made.
   b. They are discussing the possibility of building a new high school, _____ they have made no decision.
   c. The textbooks have not yet arrived, _____ have the workbooks.
   d. Helen _____ Polly will take the children to the art museum.
   e. Send the letter to Mrs. Horne, _____ she will send you the requested materials.

2. List an appropriate correlative conjunction to complete each sentence.

   a. _____ the managing partner _____ his assistant could find the error in the account.
   b. He asked _____ for suggestions _____ for volunteers.
   c. _____ Artco Printing Co. _____ Armstrong Supply Company is reliable.
   d. Please ask _____ Chuck _____ Dana to help you proofread the report.
   e. We will go _____ to Orlando _____ to Miami.

3. List an appropriate subordinating conjunction to complete each sentence.

   a. _____ you use the latest technology, your procedures will become outdated.
   b. Our staff grew _____ our sales volume increased.
   c. _____ Mr. York will be on vacation next week, we will need to work on some of his projects.
   d. We should set a date for a retreat _____ we can plan our objectives for next year.
   e. _____ you consider resigning, please discuss the situation with the human resources director.

4. List an appropriate linking adverb to complete each sentence.

   a. That word processing program is complicated; _____ , no one in the office can use it expertly at this time.
   b. We shall need additional office help soon. _____ , we plan to place an advertisement in the Sunday paper.
   c. Mrs. Mansell has made several improvements in the report. _____, she will be suggesting changes in our recommendations.
   d. Mr. Murphy will not arrive until Thursday; _____ , the conference must begin Wednesday afternoon.
   e. Complimentary tickets will be offered to regular customers. _____, they will have a choice of dates.

5. Tell whether each of the following words is a coordinating, correlative, or subordinating conjunction or a linking adverb. Then, compose a sentence containing each word.

   a. and   e. because
   b. as if   f. therefore
   c. not only, but also   g. neither, nor
   d. however   h. but

Section H

Interjections

> **Definition:**
> **Interjections** are exclamations or expressions that convey reactions to what has happened or to what has been said.

Interjections may be words or other familiar expressions.

Great!   Fantastic!   Congratulations!   Gosh!   Wow!
Yes!   Nonsense!   Gee!   Ouch!   Super!

The two most important uses of interjections are to indicate the following:

1. Listeners' approval of, agreement with, excitement about, or surprise concerning what has been said.

   OK   Certainly!   Right!   Great!   Gee!

2. Listeners' disapproval of, disagreement with, doubt about, or disappointment concerning what has been said.

   Mmmmm   Really?
   Wellll   Nonsense!

While interjections frequently occur in conversations, they seldom appear in business writing. However, communicators sometimes use interjections in advertisements and in verbatim reports of someone's reactions. When you use an interjection in a written message, place an exclamation point or a comma after the interjection.

Mrs. Gammin exclaimed, "Wow! We now have 126 new members."
Mr. Page responded, "Oh, I didn't know that was my job."

CHECK YOUR UNDERSTANDING 41

List an appropriate interjection to complete each of the following sentences. Add the necessary punctuation.

1. Gayle agreed by saying, " _____ Let's see if six companies will donate prizes for a drawing."

2. _____ in that case, I believe that I had better review the materials in the folder.
3. When Miss Moon discovered that she had a winning ticket, she grabbed her friend and shouted, " _____ ."
4. As soon as the results of the election were announced, she yelled, " _____ ."
5. Miss Dalton said, " _____ you won the award!"

Editing applications

1. List the interjections in the following sentences:

   a. Ouch! I hurt my finger.
   b. Miss Grayson said, "Well, I think we will have 35 people at the luncheon."
   c. When the home owner saw the boys running down the alley, he shouted, "Hey! Those are my tools."
   d. The travel consultant discouragingly said, "No, I doubt that you will find a lower price for the kind of trip you want to take."
   e. "Boy! How do you find time to accomplish so much?" Kim asked.
   f. Congratulations! You have been elected to the Student Council.
   g. After seeing the software demonstration, the manager said, "Well, I believe this is exactly what we need."
   h. As Susan led her children through the zoo, she suddenly yelled, "Careful! That monkey might bite you."
   i. Wow! What a beautiful day to go for a walk.
   j. When Miles received the letter from Sabo & Company inviting him for an interview, he said, "Fantastic!"
   k. The applicant commented to me, "Gee, these people are so friendly and helpful!"
   l. Fortunately, someone who noticed the truck swerving yelled, "Hey! Look out!"
   m. Mr. Tauber didn't conceal his reaction: "Wow!" he responded. "I never anticipated such cooperation!"
   n. When I reported the incident, Miss Bell was not sure what to think: "Mmmmm," she said, "we'd better discuss this matter when we have more time."
   o. The agent discouraged us: "No," he commented, "I don't think you'll find anything at such a low price."
   p. The gas station owner exclaimed, "Boy! We're selling a lot more gasoline since we lowered our price."

q. Mrs. Baylor's response to me was forceful: "Bunk! I was home all afternoon, and no service representative came to this house."

r. The representative replied, "Uhhh, I'm not sure, but I'll find out if the guarantee covers that situation."

s. Miss Sellers was dumbfounded: "Golly," she said, "I never expected to win."

t. The chairperson exclaimed, "Why! These are the best qualified applicants we have ever interviewed!"

SECTION I

Words Used as Two or More Parts of Speech

The same word can sometimes belong to more than one of the eight parts of speech. For instance, you may use some words as both nouns and verbs.

As a Noun	As a Verb
The *report* is thorough.	They *report* each week.
Our *supply* was sufficient.	You *supply* the information.
That *handle* is weak.	We *handle* clients' questions.

Report, *supply*, and *handle* are spelled the same in both the first and second columns. However, the words are used differently in the two columns. Their use determines what part of speech they belong to—noun or verb. Since the words in the left column name *things*, you should be able to recognize them as nouns.

Another way to recognize words as nouns is to consider the changes in form that the words could have in a particular use. In the left column, the italicized words are singular; however, you could change these words to their plural forms. Only nouns have this characteristic.

Use the same kind of procedure to identify the part of speech of the italicized words in the right column. Since these words name actions performed by their subjects, you may be able to identify them as verbs on this basis alone. In addition, you can change the tenses of these words from present tense to past tense. Only verbs have this characteristic.

Thus, to identify what part of speech a particular word is, first use the definitions of the parts of speech. Second, consider the changes in form that are possible for the word as the word is used in a particular sentence.

A few words can be used as more than two parts of speech. Consider the word *that*. The procedure for identifying what part of speech is involved is exactly the same.

> *That* contract is necessary. (*That* modifies *contract*; hence, in this use, *that* is an adjective.)
>
> *That* will happen soon. (*That* replaces a noun; hence, in this use, *that* is a pronoun.)
>
> We know *that* you will enjoy the conference. (*That* introduces the dependent clause "you will enjoy the conference"; hence, in this use, *that* is a subordinating conjunction.)
>
> Mrs. Farley knew the dress was *that* expensive. (*That* modifies the adjective *expensive*; hence, in this use, *that* is an adverb.)

CHECK YOUR UNDERSTANDING 42

Name the part of speech for each italicized word in the following sentences:

1. Would you please *help* Lois proofread the annual report.
2. If his employer will let him, Dave will *work* 50 hours a week.
3. We have checked the *stock* in the supply room.
4. His *work* will take him to North Carolina for three weeks.
5. We appreciated the *help* that we received during the seminar.
6. We *stock* colored index cards of all sizes.

 EDITING APPLICATIONS

1. Identify the part of speech of the italicized word in each of the following sentences:

   a. That company *gives* discount rates on large orders.
   b. *Since* Kelly drove 30 miles to buy fresh peaches, she bought some for her neighbors.
   c. When my sister came home from school, she *laid* her books on the desk.
   d. They wanted a *well-known* speaker for the opening session.
   e. *Everyone* was eager to learn who was named valedictorian.
   f. Please send *a* picture to use on the visa for Yugoslavia.
   g. Our office workers *usually* leave at 5:00 p.m.
   h. *Congratulations*! We are proud of you.
   i. My cousin sent *his* son to Princeton.

j. Do you think R. J. *or* Monty will accept?

k. The dividends *were* welcomed by the stockholders.

l. Mr. Cortez knows that good *communication* skills are important.

m. CPA stands for certified public accountant, a professional title *for* accountants.

n. Betty's grandmother sent *her* a blouse for her birthday.

o. Carelessness can cause *costly* mistakes in business.

p. The extra work will be divided between *you* and *me*.

q. All state representatives *report* the activities occurring in their states.

r. The candidate claimed *that* he would not raise taxes.

s. The *letterhead* that you had printed looks impressive.

t. The library is an excellent source for *up-to-date* information.

u. *Many* firms provide excellent educational programs for their employees.

v. She mailed her brother a package that *contained* stationery and stamps.

w. Miss Wilson, if you will put *that* on the floor, we will have more room on the table.

x. Team members *must be prepared* to offer assistance.

y. I believe that *28* new members will be initiated on Thursday.

z. Do you like *this* one as well as the red one?

aa. The colored pens were divided *among* the five children.

bb. One of the walkers wanted to increase the pace *so that* she could get more exercise.

cc. Miss Perri will explain the *wraparound* feature of the computer today.

dd. She *transferred* $2,000 from her savings account to her checking account.

ee. Mr. Woods *frequently* gives motivational presentations in schools.

ff. Tessa is *busier* than any other person I know.

gg. When Mr. Borden saw the changes, he said, "*Terrific*! Now we can finish the project on schedule."

hh. The caterer provided *not only* cups and plates *but also* knives, forks, spoons, and napkins.

ii. This flight is full, *but* another leaves in two hours.

jj. Mrs. Leverton's grandchildren hope to go to France next year; *therefore*, they are studying French.

kk. According to the *report*, production and sales have increased.

    ll.   *Neither* Miss Elko *nor* Miss Green has bought a house in Stillwater.

   mm. A *quiet* area is necessary to encourage good studying techniques.

   nn. She's trying *to locate* an inexpensive apartment.

SECTION J

Grammatical Constructions

Subjects, verbs, and direct objects are examples of grammatical constructions. The definition of most parts of speech indicates their grammatical construction or the way they are used. For example, verbs tell what the subject does, adjectives and adverbs modify other words, and prepositions and conjunctions join various elements. However, the definitions of nouns and pronouns do not indicate how these words can be used.

NOUN FUNCTIONS

Nouns and pronouns are used most frequently as a subject, direct object, indirect object, object of a preposition, noun in direct address, appositive, and predicate noun.

Subject

A noun or pronoun naming what is being discussed is the **subject** of the sentence. The subject of a verb determines whether you use a singular or plural verb. The subject also determines whether you use a first-person, second-person, or third-person verb. This correspondence between the subject and the form of the verb is called *subject-verb agreement*.

That company hires many kinds of employees.
Those companies hire many kinds of employees.

A personal pronoun serving as the subject must be in the subjective case.

She is a vice president.
They participate in the conference each year.

Direct Object

A noun or pronoun naming who or what that receives the action of a transitive verb in active voice is a **direct object.** (See Section C for information about transitive verbs and active voice.)

> The company trained those sales *representatives*.
> Customers expect excellent *service*.

A personal pronoun that is a direct object must be in the objective case.

> The editor complimented *them*.
> I evaluated *her*.

Indirect Object

A noun or pronoun naming the person or thing to whom or for whom something is sent, said, or done is an **indirect object.** You can rephrase an indirect object as the object of the preposition *to*. When you have an indirect object, you will also have a direct object.

Indirect objects occur after special transitive verbs with the meaning *send*, *tell*, or *offer*. The indirect objects are italicized in the following sentences:

> Stella sent her *mother* flowers. (To whom did Stella send flowers?)
> The company sends its *clients* attractive birthday cards. (To whom did the company send the cards?)

A personal pronoun that is an indirect object must be in the objective case.

> Ricky threw *him* the ball.

Object of a Preposition

A noun or pronoun joined to another part of a sentence by a preposition is the **object of a preposition**.

> The objective of the *message* is to sell the books.
> That officer is employed by a large *organization*.

A personal pronoun used as the object of a preposition must be in objective case.

> Elaine received a letter from *him*.

Noun in Direct Address

A noun or pronoun naming the receiver and addressed directly to that person is a **noun in direct address**. In written messages, such a noun is set off with commas.

Judith, please play the piano for us.

As you requested, *Ms. Dawson*, the meeting will be held in September.

According to our records, your dental checkup is scheduled for Friday, *Mrs. Landrum*.

Appositive

A noun renaming a noun or pronoun that it follows is an **appositive**. If the meaning of the first noun is clear even if the appositive is omitted, the appositive is a **nonrestrictive appositive** and should be set off with commas. If the meaning of the first noun is not clear when the appositive is omitted, the appositive is a **restrictive appositive** and should not be set off with commas.

> Darlene Hughes, *my friend*, read a book on effective management. (nonrestrictive)
>
> My friend *Darlene Hughes* read a book on effective management. (restrictive)

Predicate Noun

A noun or pronoun following a linking verb and renaming the subject is a **predicate noun**. A personal pronoun serving as a predicate noun should be in the subjective case.

> Ms. Smith is our *manager*.
>
> The person accountable will be *she*.

CHECK YOUR UNDERSTANDING 43

List the grammatical construction or use of each underlined word in the following sentences:

1. Marshall Howell, our building <u>supervisor</u>, sent someone to inspect the heating system.
2. Miss Moser gave her <u>class</u> an assignment on international trade.
3. After the review, the <u>editor</u> was elated.
4. The band composed three <u>songs</u> for the concert.
5. <u>Darrell</u>, do you plan to use desktop publishing in your office?
6. My brother <u>Paul</u> will enter graduate school in September.
7. The author responded to her phone <u>call</u>.
8. A conference is a <u>meeting</u>.

OTHER KINDS OF CONSTRUCTIONS

Other grammatical constructions include phrases, clauses, and sentences.

Types of Phrases

Phrases are units of two or more words that are grammatically related but that do *not* contain a subject and a verb.

There are many types of phrases. In general, phrases often consist of a main element plus related words (e.g., helping verbs, modifiers, objects). Such phrases are named after their main element. In the examples below, the main element is italicized.

the busy *manager* (noun phrase)
has been *completed* (verb phrase)
to announce the winner (infinitive phrase)
proofreading the letter, Ms. Neff . . . (participle phrase)
He likes *singing* alto (gerund phrase)
very *satisfactory* (adjective phrase)
extremely *patiently* (adverb phrase)
from the house (prepositional phrase)

CHECK YOUR UNDERSTANDING 44

Write the name of each phrase underlined in the following sentences:

1. To find someone who wants to work hard is becoming more difficult.
2. Martin will attend the university across town.
3. Speaking to a large group makes many people nervous.
4. That book has been read by most of the class.
5. Leaning over the balcony, Lee waved to the people below.
6. Our three supervisors received special awards.
7. The president of our firm arrived very early.
8. The ideas that were presented were quite basic.

Clauses

Clauses are grammatical units that include a subject and a verb. The basic types of clauses are dependent and independent clauses.

Dependent Clauses. **Dependent clauses** are introduced by relative pronouns like *who, whose, whom, which,* or *that* or by subordinating conjunctions like *as, if, since, when, because.* Dependent clauses may be noun clauses, adjective clauses, or adverb clauses.

> *Whoever signs up by 9:00 a.m.* will receive free tickets. (noun clause)
> The truth is *that an efficient secretary is invaluable.* (noun clause)
> He said *that the tailor will hem the slacks.* (noun clause)
> The lady *who drove* was very careful. (adjective clause)
> She will fly *if the fare is reasonable.* (adverb clause)
> *When the house is completed*, we will move to Denver. (adverb clause)

CHECK YOUR UNDERSTANDING 45

Identify the dependent clauses in the following sentences as noun clauses, adjective clauses, or adverb clauses:

1. Mr. Rains, *who prepares tax returns*, works late every night.
2. *Since we met our goal*, the PTA will receive $5,000.
3. We know *that the aerobics class can help you lose weight.*
4. *Whoever requested the information* will receive it soon.
5. We will discuss the project *when Kathrine calls a meeting.*

Restrictive Clauses. Dependent clauses that serve as modifiers may be either restrictive or nonrestrictive. **Restrictive clauses** are clauses that cannot be omitted without changing the meaning of a sentence. Restrictive clauses are not set off with commas. Note that the following sentences make no sense without the dependent clauses:

> The sales representative *who sells the most books* will receive a bonus.
> Anyone *who communicates effectively* has an advantage in finding employment.
> The person *who finds my watch* will receive a reward.

CHECK YOUR UNDERSTANDING 46

Rewrite the following sentences, and insert an appropriate restrictive clause in each sentence:

1. A person _____ is an interior decorator.
2. The four employees _____ will present a report to the management group.
3. Letters _____ usually are effective.

4. The girl _____ is my sister.
5. Students _____ will receive extra credit.

Nonrestrictive Clauses. **Nonrestrictive clauses** often add important information, but they may be omitted without destroying the meaning of the sentence. Nonrestrictive clauses *should* be set off by commas.

> The Botanical Garden, *which contains rare plants*, is open all year.
> David Guion, *who has an excellent musical background*, is from Texas.

Note that the meaning of the above examples is not destroyed even if the dependent clauses are omitted.

> The Botanical Garden is open all year.
> David Guion is from Texas.

CHECK YOUR UNDERSTANDING 47

Rewrite the following sentences. Underline the nonrestrictive clauses and punctuate the sentences properly.

1. Her counselor who truly cares about students is well liked.
2. My jade plant which is in the living room requires special care.
3. Seattle which has many days of rain each year is a popular city to visit.
4. Mrs. Gaynor who gave the keynote speech will leave for Michigan at 2:00 p.m.
5. Mr. Bartel who mispronounces words will lose the confidence of the audience.

Independent Clauses and Their Uses. Like dependent clauses, **independent clauses** have a subject and a verb. However, independent clauses can stand alone as sentences. When they do, they begin with a capital letter and have the appropriate sentence-end punctuation. The four kinds of sentences are simple, compound, complex, and compound-complex.

1. A simple sentence has one main thought. Even a sentence with a compound subject and a compound verb can be a simple sentence.

    That firm distributes maps of the downtown area.
    The fathers and sons will decide on the menu and will cook the meal.

2. A compound sentence has at least two independent clauses. You may join these clauses (a) with a comma and a coordinating conjunction (*and, but, or, nor*) or (b) with a semicolon without a

conjunction or with a semicolon and a linking adverb (therefore, nevertheless, however, etc.).

The problem was difficult, but Mary solved it.
Ellen lives in Dallas; Janet lives in Houston.
Coy thought he failed the test; therefore, he was surprised to see a good grade.

3. A complex sentence has one independent clause and one or more dependent clauses.

Ms. Burkhart flew to Atlanta because her clients wanted to discuss a new business venture.

4. A compound-complex sentence has two independent clauses and one dependent clause.

Margie called the ticket office; and Mrs. Penn, who is the new manager, sold her eight ballet tickets.

TABLE J-1   FOUR SENTENCE STYLES

Sentence Style	Number of Clauses	Types of Clauses
Simple	One	Independent
Compound	Two or more	All independent
Complex	Two or more	One independent and at least one dependent
Compound-Complex	Three or more	At least two independent and one dependent

CHECK YOUR UNDERSTANDING 48

Study the following sentences and identify them as simple, compound, complex, or compound-complex:

1. Mrs. Todd went to the doctor to get a shot.
2. The call came early in the morning, and I felt good about the news all day.
3. After the accountant sent the papers to the Securities and Exchange Commission, he waited five days for a response.
4. Mr. Wong and Ms. Okita select the pictures for the yearbook.
5. Please give your mileage bonus number to the travel agent; she needs it for your next trip.
6. Discount airline tickets are popular, and Consolidated Airlines has the best prices if you can purchase your ticket four weeks in advance.

Types of sentences

The three types of sentences are declarative, interrogative, or imperative. **Declarative sentences** make statements and are followed by a period.

> The new price list is being printed.
> Mr. Rege will plant the flowers Thursday.
> We enjoy our Spanish class.

Interrogative sentences ask questions and are followed by a question mark.

> Has Marsha read the article?
> Does she qualify for a loan?
> Will the director oversee the project?

Imperative sentences express commands, give directions, or make requests and are usually followed by a period.

> Turn right at the second stop sign.
> Please fill in the information requested on the form.
> Will you please send me two copies of your article. (Imperative sentence phrased as a question to sound more courteous and punctuated with a period.)

You may use an exclamation point after a statement or command to express urgency or excitement. Sentences ending with an exclamation point are called **exclamatory sentences**.

> Look at the size of that diamond!
> Roxanne is going, too!
> We leave for Europe tomorrow!

CHECK YOUR UNDERSTANDING 49

Punctuate the following sentences and tell if they are declarative, interrogative, imperative, or exclamatory:

1. Please be quiet
2. Keep your expense receipts to submit for reimbursement
3. Whom do you think will be on the school debate team
4. Criteria for selecting service representatives are dependability, promptness, and appearance
5. Are you planning to go to the conference

EDITING APPLICATIONS

1. Identify the function of the underlined words in the following sentences:

   a. Competition tends to keep prices lower in most <u>situations</u>.

b. Joel Barr, the <u>vice president</u> of Henderson Supply Company, designed the new logo for the stationery.

c. Noel seems confident that she will complete the <u>assignment</u> on time.

d. Exercising and eating correctly are <u>necessary</u> to maintain a healthy body.

e. The <u>teacher</u> gave Cindy a list of suggestions for the <u>program</u>, didn't she, <u>Stephanie</u>?

f. They sent copies to the committee <u>members</u> and Bob Spison, the <u>sponsor</u>.

g. The <u>table</u> was placed in the faculty lounge.

h. <u>Mr. Werner</u> and <u>Miss Cleary</u> are <u>dentists</u> who donate four hours a week to charity work.

i. The quarterback threw the <u>receiver</u> the <u>football</u>.

j. <u>Andrew</u>, be sure to lock the car doors.

2. Identify the type of phrase underlined in each of the following sentences:

a. The game <u>will have been played</u> before Evelyn gets home.

b. The committee wanted to make a contribution <u>to the Shelter for the Abused</u>.

c. Ben Simpson likes <u>to include</u> needy children as his guests at the annual science fair.

d. Assertiveness training enables participants <u>to identify</u> passive and aggressive behavior.

e. <u>Touring a firm's computer center</u> can stimulate student interest in computer science.

f. <u>Seeing the capabilities of a computer</u>, Dana decided that she should take a programming course.

3. Identify the following items as phrases or clauses:

a. to the movie

b. because the computer class is filled

c. among her friends

d. she is writing a report

e. down the street

f. in addition to the management consultants

g. if you graduate from college

h. since her employer rated her highly

i. because of his leadership ability

j. before Wednesday morning

4. Revise the sentences on page 72, providing the necessary punctuation. Underline the restrictive and the nonrestrictive clauses.

a. The paper that will be used in the printer is watermarked.
b. Correspondence that is not filed promptly may be lost.
c. Hazel Byron who put her career goals in writing has influenced others to investigate career opportunities.
d. The statistics that were presented at yesterday's meeting were accurate.
e. Decision-making processes which many teachers are including in their classes help students solve personal and professional problems.

5. Identify the following sentences as simple, compound, complex, or compound-complex:

a. Because he was overweight, he had to watch his diet carefully.
b. Clarity, conciseness, and courtesy are essential for an effective message.
c. Will the organizing committee have the program planned by August 1?
d. Examine the various brands carefully so that you can make an informed decision.
e. Ken was in Minneapolis and Chicago last week, and he made numerous sales in both cities.
f. Marcelle will go to a company-sponsored seminar in Austin or Albuquerque.
g. I planned to purchase her gift this week; but after I paid my bills, I didn't have enough money.
h. Stay out of that puddle!
i. Mrs. Wynn is not in the office today, but she will be back tomorrow.
j. Mr. Baker has requested that we reorganize the files and make new folders.

SECTION K

Period, Question Mark, and Exclamation Point

The period, question mark, and exclamation point are **sentence-end punctuation marks**. They separate each sentence from what follows.

Without sentence-end punctuation, readers would have to figure out where each sentence ends and the next one begins.

PERIOD

Use a period in the following ways:

1. After every declarative sentence

   The operating instructions for the printer are easy to understand.
   Present the sales receipt if you return the merchandise.

   Use only one period even if it serves more than one purpose.

   We ordered storage cases for the disks from McClellan and Co.

2. After most imperative sentences

   Please complete the form and return it to this office.
   If you decide to run, send the entry fee to John Lee.
   Please tell me about your trip.

3. After indirect questions.(Indirect questions report what someone asked; they do not call for an answer.)

   Weldon asked when he could have his car repaired.
   Miss Osho questioned whether the store had enough sales personnel.

4. After interrogative sentences that are really commands or instructions. These are frequently called courteous requests and ask for action.

   Will you please send me five copies of the report.
   Will you also reserve a car for me in Tulsa.
   Would you please send invitations to the people in the human resources department.

5. After initials and most abbreviations

Mrs. Rosemary M. Popkin	Jr.
M.B.A.	Inc.
Ph.D.	ea.
a.m.	no.

   Many abbreviations consisting of several capitalized initial letters are written without periods or spacing. Follow the practice of the organization involved.

   IRS = Internal Revenue Service
   AT&T = American Telephone and Telegraph Co.

GE = General Electric Co.
CPA = Certified Public Accountant
CPS = Certified Professional Secretary

Omit periods after two-letter state abbreviations.

CA = California   NY = New York   TX = Texas

6. Between dollars and cents expressed in figures. In expressing even dollar amounts, omit the period and zeroes.

That compact disk player costs $786.37.
The telephone bill for last month was $123, but that included 26 long distance calls.

7. After each number or letter designating items in a list or outline.

1. tomatoes
2. beans
3. potatoes

CHECK YOUR UNDERSTANDING 50

Rewrite the following sentences, and supply periods as necessary:

1. Mr B T Batson, the assistant to Mr Doug P Walker of Blackmon Professional Services, Inc, will receive his Ph D next week
2. Lt Col Dale C Styles will leave from Albany at 3:45 p m on Westport Airlines Flight No 552
3. Dr Carl T Ward will give the keynote address for the Martha V Allen Symposium at 10:00 a m in Building No 2
4. Mr Tyree and Mr Owens work as distributors for Radix & Co
5. Fran Parker, CPS, met with Mrs Genna Lane at 1:30 p m on October 12 in the counselor's office

---

QUESTION MARK

Use a question mark in the following ways:

1. After each direct question. These questions usually require a response of some type. (Do not use a question mark after indirect questions or after commands or instructions phrased as questions. See Items 3 and 4 under "Period" on page 73.)

When is the mortgage payment due?
Will the payments be distributed this week?

2. After a quoted statement to indicate the speaker's doubt or disbelief concerning what was said.

Ms. Lidster responded, "The agreement was *not* signed?"

We heard Jackson's pleased reaction: "Do you mean that the school will pay for the *whole* trip?"

3. After each term that raises a question in a sentence containing a series of questions. In such a series, use lowercase letters for the word after each question mark.

Miss Leggett needs answers to the following questions: when are you coming? where are you staying? do you need transportation?

She asked, "Do you enjoy plays? rock concerts? symphony concerts? opera? ballet?

EXCLAMATION POINT

Exclamation points are seldom used in business messages except in advertisements, where they may suggest delight, surprise, or excitement. Occasionally, you may use exclamation points to report or convey reactions in other kinds of messages.

Miss Knowles received a $2,000 bonus at the end of the year! Wait! Slow down! We don't need to be there till 7:00 p.m.

CHECK YOUR UNDERSTANDING 51

Rewrite the following sentences, and insert periods, question marks, and exclamation points as necessary:

1. I have four questions for you: Will the plant bloom all summer Is it a perennial Does it require much water Does it grow very tall
2. Mr Mercley asked, "Did she receive her Ph D degree in May "
3. Mr Kenwood proudly exclaimed, "We have finally found an efficient administrative assistant "
4. Would you please send Mr Hyatt, Ms Jarmon, and Miss Hill travel brochures on England, Scotland, and Ireland
5. Mr Fairchild asked whether we planned to merge with T M Haskell and Co

---

EDITING APPLICATIONS

1. Revise the sentences on page 76, inserting periods, question marks, and exclamation points as necessary.

    a. Would you please ask Millie to substitute for me on October 11
    b. Don't you dare put that snake on me
    c. The Fowler Health Associates, Inc, of Anchorage, Alaska, will receive a $6,000 grant in June
    d. Hugh asked if he could examine the records of their clients in Fort Collins
    e. Would May 9 be a good date for us to tour your communication center
    f. Finally, the interest rate on the savings account is increasing
    g. Would you please send me two cases of paper towels
    h. Go ahead and submit the papers required to enter the MBA program at the University of St Louis
    i. Please credit Harley Flanagin's account for the returned merchandise
    j. Please bring three items for the sale

2. Revise the following paragraphs, inserting the needed periods, question marks, and exclamation points:

The quarterly board meeting of the Fort McHenry Teachers Association was held in the conference room of Addison More, Inc, on Monday, March 25

As the first order of business, the president, Ms Joan S Murray, asked, "What do you believe causes student absenteeism" Ideas that surfaced included illness, lack of interest, and lack of encouragement

She then asked how teachers could help students improve their attendance Several people responded with similar ideas Teach students more about proper diet and exercise Relate lessons to topics of student interest Communicate with parents Praise something about each student every day

3. Revise the following sentences, inserting the proper punctuation:
    a. Can you send us apples and oranges
    b. She is extremely qualified for the position; she has had six years' experience at W C Dodson & Co
    c. Are you going to Mexico by car by plane or by bus
    d. If you want the dishes, buy them from H K Steakly, Inc for $75 before 5:00 pm Saturday
    e. Mary Hausley, CPS, won a two-week vacation as a prize
    f. Ann suddenly exclaimed, "I won I won "

SECTION L

Comma, Semicolon, and Colon

Sentence-end punctuation separates sentences and indicates completion of a thought unit. **Internal punctuation** sets off words, phrases, or clauses to clarify their relationships.

COMMA

Use a comma in the following ways:

1. Before a coordinating conjunction (*and, but, or, nor*) that joins the independent clauses of a compound sentence

    The students planned the honors ceremony, and their parents enjoyed it.
    Houses are selling better now, but how long will that last?
    Her assistant will personally deliver the message to her, or he will send the message with someone else.

2. To separate three or more items in a series

    Karen is taking math, English, and history this semester.
    Walking more, eating less, and reducing stress can help a person lose weight.
    Rita asked him to revise, proofread, copy, and distribute the report.

3. After introductory expressions

    Because correct grammar usage is so important, every student should study grammar diligently.
    To have the beautiful yard, Mr. Crowley worked many hours.
    While visiting her grandmother, Diana heard many stories about events that happened 60 years ago.
    Confident, Mrs. Kamens submitted several suggestions.

4. To set off nonrestrictive elements

    Dillon, which is in the mountains, has a dry climate.
    The procedures manual, which was written four years ago, should be updated.

Mr. Finley, Ms. Glasgow's supervisor, nominated her for a scholarship.

Her new book, *How to Buy Stocks and Prosper*, is selling well.

In deciding whether to set off *Inc.* and *Ltd.* after company names, follow the practice of the firm involved.

Moreland Plumbing, Inc., bid on 20 houses.
Shelton Tackett, Ltd., sells cashmere sweaters.
Lindsey Foust Inc. made the arrangements.

5. Around transitional and parenthetical expressions

He knows, however, that the design will work.
The purpose of the catalog, therefore, is to simplify ordering supplies.
Her suggestion, in my opinion, was excellent.

6. After the first of two equal-ranking adjectives. Equal-ranking adjectives can be joined by *and*. Do not use a comma if the two adjectives cannot be joined by *and*.

She is a generous, outgoing person.
Extend a courteous, pleasant greeting to each customer.
The company published and distributed its annual financial report.

7. After introductions to short direct quotations

Miss Cox stated, "Everyone should have a savings account."
The director said, "Close your eyes and let your imagination take over."
Mr. NcNutt asked, "Will you have the report completed by tonight?"

8. Around nouns in direct address

Ester, the poster that you painted is beautiful.
If you will supply us with the information, Mr. Shelton, we will prepare your resume.
Try this adjustable chair, Miss Linder, and see if it is comfortable.

9. At the point where something is omitted in a pair of parallel constructions

Mr. Newlin ate the baked chicken; Mr. Brown, the baked fish.
Dresses in this department will sell for $49.95; dresses in the teens department, for $29.95.
The human resources director analyzed the application; the administrative assistant, the written tests.

CHECK YOUR UNDERSTANDING 52

Rewrite the following sentences, and insert commas as necessary:

1. The assistant manager Miss Jo Maddy said "We have three vacancies in our office and we plan to fill them by Monday."
2. Because sales have increased Sperry Electronics has increased the size of its operations.
3. She said however that Mr. Alton is a pleasant enthusiastic person.
4. Ruth we drove the van to the game; the Harrises the motor home.
5. We purchased these two pictures which are reproductions last month.

SEMICOLON

Use a semicolon in the following ways:

1. In compound sentences, between independent clauses not joined by a coordinating conjunction

   The Wichita City Council voted to increase the sales tax; it voted to leave the property tax unchanged.
   Using the computer for the communication course saves student time; they can edit their messages as they compose.
   The students were studying in China; therefore, they enjoyed the Chinese exhibit.
   The trees were planted last week; the landscaper, however, decided to wait another week before planting the shrubs.

2. Between items in a series if one or more items in the series contain commas

   The Andersons have purchased the store, which is in a good location; have increased its size; and have added more products.
   Mr. Trend wrote a book; submitted it to a review board, which consisted of five members; and won the top award.

   We will visit Boise, Idaho; Cheyenne, Wyoming; and Wichita, Kansas.

3. Before transitions such as *for example* and *namely* when they are used to introduce a list

   Kenneth received much advice about selecting a college; for example, check the reputation of the department in which you want to study, check the housing facilities, and check the possibility of obtaining a work scholarship.

CHECK YOUR UNDERSTANDING 53

Rewrite the following sentences, and insert semicolons as appropriate:

1. Ergonomics should be included in the course content however, it is frequently omitted.
2. The company grew rapidly the sales force increased also.
3. Mr. Greer has a meeting with Miss Pearce at 9:00 a.m. on Wednesday he plans, therefore, to return from his trip to Provo, Utah Reno, Nevada and Santa Fe, New Mexico on Tuesday.
4. Many of the managers give excellent presentations some of them, however, need more practice using audiovisual aids.
5. The review board listed several reasons for example, increasing taxes, increasing costs, and decreasing sales.

COLON

Colons are marks of anticipation. They come at the end of independent clauses and point to what follows. Use a colon in the following ways:

1. After an independent clause in a compound sentence to point to a second independent clause that provides more specific information. To emphasize the second clause, you may begin it with a capital letter.

   Technology supplies the classroom with valuable teaching devices: The video camera and VCR provide fascinating opportunities for students.
   We believe that the shorter hours are practical: The largest crowd comes at 6:00 p.m.
   The basketball star pleased his fans: He signed autographs for an hour after the game.

2. After an independent clause containing words like *following* or *these* that introduces a list.

   Educational technology provide the following advantages: enhanced instruction, enriched lessons, increased student interest, and improved learning.
   Please send us these items: two reams of bond paper, four legal pads, and a box of folders.

3. After an independent clause as a formal introduction to a quotation.

   The council member announced: "The newly constructed road will be opened on May 27."
   Dr. Kirksy issued this statement: "Mark Lane is resting comfortably after the four-hour operation and should recover completely."

4. Between hours and minutes when times are expressed in figures.

   The store opens at 8:30 a.m.

5. After the salutation in letters using mixed punctuation. (See Unit 5 for information about letter formats.)

   Dear Mr. Appleton:

CHECK YOUR UNDERSTANDING 54

Rewrite the following sentences, and insert colons as appropriate:

1. Voting registration is scheduled for the following dates October 4, 5, and 6.
2. Mr. Canton made the following announcement at the meeting "Jerry Sears is our newest partner."
3. If you have your car at the service department by 730 a.m., we will complete the repairs by noon.
4. We have two vacation spots to consider Mexico and Hawaii.
5. The firm has an ambitious plan It will sell franchises in four states.

EDITING APPLICATIONS

1. Revise the following sentences, inserting needed commas:
   a. The editor the publisher and the reporter will attend the city's birthday celebration.
   b. Walking down the street Miss Booker greeted her friends with a smile.
   c. He is however an industrious well-educated individual.
   d. Becki Brandt who is valedictorian of her class plans to attend Scott University.

    e. Since the sun was shining we decided to take the boat to the lake.

    f. I know however that his attitude and behavior influenced her decision.

2. Revise the following sentences, inserting needed semicolons:

    a. Many people attended the symphony they thought that the musical selections were outstanding.

    b. Janice Moore is the new receptionist she already knows everyone's name and extension number.

    c. Ralph conducts one-hour tours of the museum however, he believes the tour should be scheduled for two hours.

    d. Mrs. Raney received many suggestions for example, to increase the number of reference books, to increase the library's hours, and to hire an assistant.

    e. Bill will give the same presentation in Miami, Florida New Orleans, Louisiana and Little Rock, Arkansas.

3. Revise the following sentences, inserting needed colons:

    a. Mrs. Howell made the following statement to her department members "We must improve the quality of our products immediately."

    b. My flight leaves at 930 a.m. and arrives at 1142 a.m.

    c. We have two options we can meet in Dallas, or we can meet in New York City.

    d. The gardener explained why the grass was turning yellow It was not getting sufficient water.

    e. Mr. Gladstone used the following salutation in his letter *Dear Mrs. Hadley*.

4. Revise the following sentences, inserting needed commas, semicolons, and colons:

    a. To improve staff morale Mrs. Hardy plans to hire a consultant to conduct three workshops.

    b. Please send the financial report to the following people Jack Madison Don Potect and Deborah Isley.

    c. The English department wants an instructor who has good rapport with students therefore they will thoroughly check any applicant's references.

    d. To succeed in the graduate program you must have ambition interest and intelligence.

    e. Tamara is taking a computer class therefore she wants to buy a computer to use at home.

SECTION M

Quotation Marks, Dashes, Parentheses, and Brackets

This section deals with punctuation marks that work primarily in pairs, enclosing one or more words, phrases, or clauses. Use quotation marks primarily to indicate the use of someone else's exact words. Use dashes, parentheses, and brackets to punctuate material that is not essential but may be helpful. (See Section O for information about rules of order and spacing for quotation marks, dashes, parentheses, and brackets.)

QUOTATION MARKS

Use quotation marks around the following items:

1. Direct quotations unless they are single spaced and indented from both margins to indicate that the material is directly quoted from a document. **Direct quotations** are the exact words of a person. **Indirect quotations** express the same meaning in different words and are not enclosed in quotation marks.

    Mrs. Moyer said, "I will be happy to serve as the chairperson for the fund drive."
    Mrs. Moyer said that she would be happy to serve as the chairperson for the fund drive.

    Follow these guidelines in using quotation marks for direct quotations:

    a. If the quotation is interrupted by other words, enclose both segments of the quotation in quotation marks.

    "We need to read the nutrition labels on foods," Lavina said, "so that we can prepare healthier meals for our families."

    b. Use single quotation marks around a quotation *within* a quotation.

    He said, "If a box is marked 'Handle with Care,' please give the box to Mr. Morsely."

    c. In a quotation containing several sentences, use quotation marks before the first sentence and after the last. In a quotation containing several paragraphs, use quotation marks before each paragraph but *after* only the last paragraph.

2. Definitions

    A *legal back* is "a cover that is somewhat heavier and larger than the paper on which a legal document is keyed."

3. The titles of parts, chapters, or other sections of books, pamphlets, reports, periodicals, and newspapers. Underline or set in italics titles of separately published works.

    Chapter 3, "Writing Better Letters," in Mr. Loft's newest book, *Communicating in Business*, provides many excellent suggestions. Be sure to read Miss Barker's article "Entrepreneurship Opportunities" in the April issue of *Progress*.

4. Cited words or expressions and elements given as examples. If the citations or examples are only a few words in length, italics or underlining are often preferred to quotation marks.

    The word "accommodate" is often misspelled.
    The following sentence illustrates a restrictive clause: "A person who works hard will succeed."

5. Slang or other expressions that are inappropriate for the message

    Craig said the plan is a "bummer."
    The girls thought the worm farm was really "gross."

CHECK YOUR UNDERSTANDING 55

Rewrite the following sentences, and insert quotation marks as appropriate:

1. President Gaines said Somewhere in the information on the plaque, use the word exemplary to describe her as an outstanding teacher.
2. The doctor said, You must follow my instructions immediately.
3. The chapter entitled Managing with Ease in *Managing Day by Day* contains numerous practical suggestions.
4. Carefully consider Mrs. Anco's statement: Learn the basic skills now and continually practice them.
5. She completely changed the personality of her family room by adding those pictures.

DASH (USED ALONE AND IN PAIRS)

In some situations, you may substitute a dash for a comma, semicolon, or colon. Use such substitutions infrequently. (Key a dash with two hyphens and no space before or after.)

Use the dash in the following ways:

1. Before one or more examples at the end of a sentence. In this use, the dash replaces a colon or semicolon.

    Yes, these people will work hard—Susan Highler, Bob Drury, and Nancy Klein.
    The chairperson made several requests of the committee—namely, to work hard, to contact many businesses, and to collect many pledges.
    The nutritionist gave three suggestions for healthy living—eat fresh vegetables, eat foods with less fat and fewer calories, and exercise daily.

2. Around parenthetical material. In this use, dashes provide greater separation than commas, but less than parentheses.

    Five other committee members agreed to Hilda's first reaction—that the color was too bright.
    Those who will report next Friday—Jan Nardine and Mack Waller—will need an overhead projector.
    Charles Brosh—based on an article in the November 5 issue of *Job Hunting*—has had much success with his job-search techniques.

CHECK YOUR UNDERSTANDING 56

Rewrite the following sentences, and supply dashes as appropriate:

1. The paper listed the three types of music that will be performed at the summer festival jazz, pop, and classical.
2. The hardware store will place carpentry tools hammers, levels, and drills on sale next week.
3. Her first thought that the water was too deep to drive through was correct.
4. The president's point that the cost was too high was easy to understand.
5. Mr. Nolen listed several rewards of leadership working with other leaders, effecting changes, and extending intellectual and professional horizons.

PARENTHESES

Parentheses are the standard way to set off supplementary information in a sentence. Such information may include references, details, and interpretative comments. Parentheses often de-emphasize the material they set off.

Use parentheses around the following items:

1. Details, examples, and other explanatory material

   Since we shipped the chairs yesterday (Monday), you should receive them by Thursday.
   The number of bankruptcies this year (see Figure 4, page 21) has greatly affected employment.
   One of Mother's arguments (that rest and relaxation are important before a test) is valid.

2. Figures or signs clarifying information in words

   The price he will charge to draw up the will is One Hundred Fifty-Five Dollars and Eighty-Five Cents ($155.85). (This form is used primarily in legal documents.)
   Did you know that even-numbered highways in the U.S. run east and west (e.g., Interstate 20).
   Some companies use the ampersand (&) in their names.

3. Numbers or letters identifying items in paragraphs

   Please consider (a) the width of the dresser, (b) the height of the lamp, and (c) the color of the wood finish.
   The three classes of verbs are (1) transitive, (2) intransitive, and (3) linking.

CHECK YOUR UNDERSTANDING 57

Rewrite the following sentences, and insert parentheses as appropriate:

1. The sketch of the monument see Drawing 4, page 37 is extremely detailed.
2. We will meet in Oklahoma City because this city offers 1 convenience, 2 low cost hotel rooms, and 3 sight-seeing opportunities.
3. We sent his company a check for Ten Thousand Five Hundred Forty-Five Dollars and Thirty-Two Cents $10,545.32.
4. I'm asking three students they will be here to serve on the committee.
5. Several tables in the book No. 15, No. 23, and No. 44 explain the factors affecting productivity.

BRACKETS

Use brackets around the following items:

1. Parenthetical insertions in material already in parentheses

Please revise Unit 7 (especially the examples that illustrate thank-you letters [i.e., pages 120-123]).

2. Expressions inserted in another person's writing

Mr. Dobson stated, "I don't care what affect [sic] this has, I don't want higher taxes." (*Sic* means that the error was contained in the original material.)

The directions state: "Remove the plug from the outlet *before* [my italics] removing the blade from the food processor."

CHECK YOUR UNDERSTANDING 58

Rewrite the following sentences, and insert brackets as appropriate:

1. Please review Chapter 3 of *Taxes for All* (especially the tables pages 30-35) so that we can discuss them with the author.
2. She concluded her notes to the secretary: "The Library Board will meet Monday, June 23, June 24 to discuss constructing a new building and hiring more help."
3. The economy will improve (that is the forecast that was published in *The Future* April 12, 19-- on pages 22-23), and business transactions should increase.
4. In the interview, the woman responded: "Today we are doing more work with less fewer employees."
5. The director's letter contained the following request: "Please send me <u>five</u> my underlining employees who are management trainee prospects."

 EDITING APPLICATIONS

1. Revise the following sentences, inserting quotation marks as appropriate:

   a. The student asked, When is the ten-page report due?
   b. The customer replied, But I have the bill on which you stamped Paid, so my account should be balanced.
   c. In economics, students are advised to make choices that produce the greatest benefits.

      d.   Actually, Louise responded, that was the most beneficial, professional seminar I have ever attended.

      e.   Ways to Improve Your Memory is the title of his article that was published in *Success*.

2.   Revise the following sentences, inserting dashes as appropriate:

      a.   When buying a house, remember some of the future costs insurance, utilities, and maintenance and repairs.

      b.   The typographical errors that I found four on the second page illustrate the importance of careful proofreading.

      c.   When I visited some cities Austin, London, New York, Miami I toured many historical sites.

      d.   The supervisor requested two reports a project status report and an expense report.

      e.   Place exact postage no more and no less on parcels going to Europe.

3.   Revise the following sentences, inserting parentheses and brackets as appropriate:

      a.   I reviewed your memo one that was dated March 8 I think, and I agree with your reasoning.

      b.   After graduation from college, Margaret will start working if you think of traveling as work for Midwest Travel Agency.

      c.   We will discuss Chapter 8 especially the parts of speech i.e., pages 25 through 30 and the functions of words next week.

      d.   When asked how she felt, Mrs. Stockly replied, "I do not feel very good well."

      e.   The managers discussed the question yesterday Wednesday; therefore, an answer should be forthcoming.

4.   Revise the following sentences, inserting quotation marks, dashes, parentheses, and brackets as appropriate:

      a.   Jason Thrasher he used to have his own printing business is now the sales manager for Fast Print.

      b.   The directions state: Put the proceeds from the sale in the envelope marked Christmas Funds <u>immediately</u> my underlining following the sale.

      c.   David said, The election for the office of president will be held on June 1.

      d.   Mrs. Witt's response that she loves to work with people and to help them in any way she can favorably impressed the interviewer.

      e.   Hugh Jeffries wrote an article entitled Money in the Marketing Process; the article was published in *Economics Today*.

SECTION N

Underlining, Omission Marks, Apostrophes, and Hyphens

This section deals with the remaining punctuation marks, all of which relate to special situations. Such situations include cited expressions, incomplete quotations, possessive and contracted forms, and separate words made into compounds. Use these marks correctly for effective messages.

UNDERLINING (ITALICS)

Underlining in keyboarded material is equivalent to italics in print. The principal use of underlining is to indicate that underlined words are titles or names of certain kinds of things.

Use underlining for the following items:

1. Titles of all separately published or separately issued works. Such works include books; sets of books, such as encyclopedias; collections of documents; pamphlets; periodicals; and newspapers as well as separately bound reports and studies. Also underline titles of movies, plays, musicals, operas, television shows, paintings, and pieces of sculpture.

   Students should set aside time each week to read magazines and newspapers like Forbes, Fortune, Business Week, The Wall Street Journal.
   Have you seen the movie Amadeus?

2. Proper names of individual craft (e.g., space shuttles, airplanes, ships, and trains)

   Eliah Jones named his private jet The Lisa.
   Their company organizes the food, entertainment, and accommodations for cruises on The Princess.

3. Letters, symbols, words, and expressions that are cited or defined including foreign words and phrases

Interpersonal skills are skills needed to live and work effectively with others.

A contract is a binding agreement between two or more persons or parties.

CHECK YOUR UNDERSTANDING 59

Rewrite the following sentences, and underline words and phrases that could also be printed in italics:

1. Accommodate and recommend are two frequently misspelled words.
2. Roget's Thesaurus is a source of synonyms and antonyms.
3. Expressions such as please, thank you, and you're welcome promote goodwill.
4. Personal Computing often publishes ratings of software programs.
5. Jim Pilmer nicknamed his Lear Jet Honey.

OMISSION MARKS

Accuracy in quotations is indispensable in effective messages. Omissions can change the meaning of any quotation and may seriously mislead the reader. Therefore, you must indicate whenever you leave anything out of a quoted sentence or passage.

Omission marks—also called **ellipsis**—are three periods, usually with one space before and after each period. Place omission marks at the point in the sentence where the omission occurs. If the omission coincides with the end of a sentence, add a space and a fourth period.

> The new policy manual states: "Employees . . . must file all insurance forms before the company will issue a check."
> The dietitian said, "During the past five years, we have seen substantial changes in eating habits . . . . "

APOSTROPHE

The placement of apostrophes requires concentration. Their proper use requires correct answers to these questions: Does the word or expression require an apostrophe? If so, where should you place the apostrophe? Use the apostrophe:

1. To form the possessive of nouns and of pronouns except *my/mine, our/ours, your/yours, his/hers/its, their/theirs,* and *whose.* (See Sections A and B, pages 1-19, for information about possessive case.)

2. To indicate omission of one or more letters in a contraction. The most commonly contracted forms are helping verbs with personal pronouns, helping verbs with *not*, and *let's* for *let us*.

Contractions of Personal Pronouns and Helping Verbs			Contractions of Helping Verbs and *Not*		
he'll	=	he will	aren't	=	are not
he's	=	he is	can't	=	cannot
I'm	=	I am	couldn't	=	could not
I'll	=	I will	doesn't	=	does not
it'll	=	it will	don't	=	do not
it's	=	it is/has	hasn't	=	has not
I've	=	I have	haven't	=	have not
she'll	=	she will	isn't	=	is not
she's	=	she is/has	shouldn't	=	should not
they'll	=	they will	wasn't	=	was not
they're	=	they are	weren't	=	were not
they've	=	they have	won't	=	will not
we're	=	we are	wouldn't	=	would not
we've	=	we have			
we'll	=	we will			
you're	=	you are			
you've	=	you have			
you'll	=	you will			

3. To form the plural of letters, numbers, symbols, abbreviations, and cited words when confusion might result if the apostrophe were omitted. Note that no confusion occurs in such forms as *M.B.A.*s or *9*s. If one item requires use of an apostrophe for clarity, use apostrophes for all similar items in that context.

> Julie already knows her ABCs.
> Be careful in distinguishing between *a*'s and *an*'s.
> Music from the 1950s is popular.

CHECK YOUR UNDERSTANDING 60

Rewrite the following sentences, and insert apostrophes as appropriate:

1. The company gave its approval for the contribution and indicated that itll be happy to lend its display of clothes from the 1930s.
2. The five CPAs said that theyll conduct the seminar on the new tax laws.

3. If you havent registered to vote, remember to do so before the deadline. Its your responsibility.
4. The responsibility for reserving a meeting place and planning the program is Jacks and yours.

HYPHEN

Use the hyphen to divide words and to form compound words. Use a hyphen in the following ways:

1. Usually after these prefixes: *ex-*, *half-*, *self-*, and *vice-*

    ex-president   self-supporting
    half-dollar   vice-chancellor (but *vice admiral*)

2. Usually *not* after these prefixes: *anti-*, *co-*, *extra-*, *post-*, *pre-*, *pro-*, and *re-*

    antibody   prejudge
    coaxial cable   pronuclear
    extracurricular   reacquaint
    postwar

3. For joining compound adjectives preceding the modified noun (See Section D, pages 38-39, for information about compound adjectives.)

4. Between compound numbers from twenty-one to ninety-nine when written in words

    Thirty-eight dollars
    Seventy-four people

5. Between the numerator and the denominator of a fraction written in words unless one part (the numerator or denominator) already contains a hyphen

    three-eighths   nine-tenths   one sixty-fourth

CHECK YOUR UNDERSTANDING 61

Rewrite the following sentences, and insert hyphens as appropriate:

1. As ex president, you will be responsible for securing officer candidates next year.
2. Senator elect Todd will speak Tuesday at 8:00 p.m. in the auditorium.

3.   You have more up to date equipment than any other school in the district; therefore, you will receive only two thirds of the amount you requested for equipment.

4.   We will divide the money raised from the telethon among the twenty two charities.

EDITING APPLICATIONS

1.   Revise the following sentences, inserting underlining as appropriate:

   a.   Wasn't last night's performance of the musical Singing in the Rain marvelous?

   b.   Be sure to read the article entitled "Marketing Strategies" in the July issue of Computer Digest.

   c.   Mr. Clancy highly recommended The Wall Street Journal and The New York Times.

   d.   Mr. and Mrs. Monroe will leave next Wednesday for a cruise on the U.S.S. Norway.

   e.   Watch for the words am, is, are, was, were, been, and be when you are asked to identify linking verbs.

2.   Revise the following sentences, inserting apostrophes as appropriate:

   a.   The four YMCAs in the area are organizing a large tournament.

   b.   When you move to a new area, its your responsibility to make social contacts.

   c.   We selected a printer with graphics capability; the Marshalls want that feature on theirs, too.

   d.   Thats a favorite topic of ours because its vital to career success.

   e.   Lets put our money in a six-month certificate of deposit; I think the interest rate is fair, dont you?

   f.   Remember that *accommodate* has two cs and two ms, but *recommend* has only one c and two ms.

   g.   Ive purchased the seeds, but its too early to plant vegetables in the garden.

   h.   Shes happy that she doesnt have to take the test tomorrow.

   i.   Weve paid our insurance premium, but Im not sure that the Browns have paid theirs.

   j.   If were going on the school trip, well have to leave home by 7:00 a.m.

3. Revise the following sentences, inserting omission marks and hyphens as appropriate:

   a. A full page ad in a magazine can cost thousands of dollars; but if the ad is eye catching, it can increase sales enough to cover the cost.

   b. The company report states "the company succeeded in buying three agencies."

   c. To amend the bylaws, a two thirds majority of the board members present is required.

   d. Denny drove faster than the posted 35 mile an hour speed limit to the interview for a part time job.

SECTION O

Rules of Order and Spacing for Punctuation Marks

ORDER OF PUNCTUATION MARKS

Two or more punctuation marks sometimes occur next to one another in a sentence. Use the following guidelines for the order of succeeding punctuation marks:

1. Place a period following an abbreviation *before* any other punctuation mark. If the abbreviation ends a declarative sentence, use only one period.

   In May, Miss Staci M. Scott, CPS, completes her M.B.A.; she is our office manager.
   The first session will start at 9:00 a.m., and the last session will begin at 4:15 p.m.

2. Place a comma or period *inside* closing quotation marks. Place a semicolon or colon *outside* closing quotation marks. Place a question mark or exclamation mark *inside* closing quotation marks if it punctuates the quotation, *outside* if it does not.

   "The employees were happy about the strike settlement," *The Denver Post* reported, "and they were eager to return to work";

moreover, the *Post* said, "they . . . wanted to start work an hour after the strike ended."

For a quotation containing a quotation, use standard quotation marks for the *enclosing* quotation and single quotation marks for the *enclosed* quotation.

Mrs. Leaverton said, *"The Professional Outlook* contains Ida Robinson's article 'The Decision-Making Process.'"
Did Mrs. Leaverton say, *"The Professional Outlook* contains Ida Robinson's article 'The Decision-Making Process'"?
Miss Bergman asked, "Have you read Ida Robinson's article 'The Decision-Making Process'?"
Mr. Perry said, "Before our next class, please read J. D. Patton's newest article, 'What Are You Going to Do with the Rest of Your Life?'"

3.   Place a punctuation mark *inside* a closing parenthesis if it punctuates the parenthetical material, *outside* if it does not.

The report contains recommendations. (See page 8.)
Please plan to stay with us (we are only seven miles from the airport) the next time you come to Phoenix.
My new computer does everything (don't you want one like it?).
Because it was raining, Ryan drove me to the airport (much to my relief!).

CHECK YOUR UNDERSTANDING 62

Rewrite the following sentences, and correct the order of punctuation marks as appropriate:

1.   Your first interview with the student will begin at 8:30 a.m., and the second interview will be at 10:00 a.m. .

2.   Reprints are now available of Edna Young's article, "Planning and Facilitating Meetings;" anyone who wants to receive a copy of this reprint or of her earlier article, "Making Airline Reservations the Electronic Way", may call me at 555-1246.

3.   Mr. O'Brien asked, "Have you discussed the article 'Electronic Mail and Calendars' with Mr. Miller"?

4.   Miss Wynne said, "Please read the article on physical fitness in the *Morning Times*".

5.   As Michael was walking to English class, he yelled, "Congratulations, Nedra, on becoming class president"!

SPACING OF PUNCTUATION MARKS

Follow these guidelines for spacing punctuation marks when keying messages:

1. Space twice after any punctuation mark at the *end* of a sentence.

   Mrs. Cosbin entered her paintings in the art show. She has several beautiful landscapes.
   Will the firm pay for the class trips? Yes, but you must meet certain requirements.

2. Within a sentence, space twice after a *colon* (except in a time designation).

   Miss Hale responded: "The membership is up 20 percent this year."
   She gave these reasons: better diet, more exercise, and less stress.
   The seminar on public relations will start at 9:30 a.m.

3. Space twice after the period that is placed after a number or letter, as in a list or outline.

   The new cars have several special features such as the following:

   1. No-lock brakes
   2. Mileage computers
   3. Electronic door locks

4. Do not space after the following punctuation marks:
   a. A period used as a decimal

      He had 95.8 percent of the answers correct.

   b. A period that is followed by a comma, semicolon, colon, question mark, or exclamation point

   Susan has an interview with a major communication firm at 2:30 p.m., and she is well prepared for it.

   c. A period used between parts of an abbreviation (e.g., M.B.A.). However, space once after a period at the *end* of any abbreviation and space once after periods following initials in a proper name.

      J. J. Harper has an M.B.A. degree.

5. Do not space before or after a dash or hyphen.

   The short-term loan will help her establish credit—an aspect of personal finance.

6. Do not space *after* an initial quotation mark, parenthesis, or bracket. Do not space *before* a closing quotation mark, parenthesis, or bracket.

Several large cities located in the northern part of the country (see Map 4, page 12) have rapid transit systems.

CHECK YOUR UNDERSTANDING 63

Rewrite the following sentences, and use correct spacing for all punctuation marks:

1. Keller Savings and Loan,located at 1405 Adams,issued notices that read as follows: "All IRA contributions must be made before April 15."
2. Kathleen asked,"Are you familiar with electronic fund transfers, Mr. Martinez?" "No," he replied, "what are they?"
3. Sandra Norwood will receive her Ph. D. degree in chemistry from Mitchell University on Saturday. I believe the ceremony begins at 1: 30 p.m.
4. L.R. Jenkins asked the following people to conduct the reprographics seminar: (1)Madylyn Parr, (2)Luciano Marici, and (3)Harewood Normin.
5. The highest grade point averages for the semester are 98.4,97.8,94.3, and 93. 5.

EDITING APPLICATIONS

1. Revise the following sentences, correcting the order and use of punctuation marks:

    a. Mrs. Rosemary Ashley, CPS, encouraged all the students by saying, "Increase your 'word power' by reading more and by making your own vocabulary list to study each week".
    b. The results of the survey are in the booklet (pages 12-14.).
    c. Miss Burnham asked the new office employees, "How many office safety hazards can you identify"?
    d. The marketing manager said, "The training conference will be in Oklahoma City on July 18; however, you must be there by 3:00 p.m. on July 17".
    e. The teacher said, "You should be able to explain the difference between *affect* and *effect*;" moreover, she continued, "you should *practice* using them"!

f.   Did Mr Ross say; "I'll help you any way I can?"

g.   If Ms Hall arrives at 9:30 a.m,. send her to my office at 9:45 a.m. .

h.   The director asked, "When was that report submitted"?

i.   Miss. Williams said that profits increased by $200000 e.g, (by 5 percent.)

j.   Her report includes the following recommendation; "Hire two additional administrative assistants". (See page 12).

2.   Revise the following sentences, spacing each punctuation mark correctly:

a.   Mr. O.L. Kotzwick, who is the ex-president, will give a presentation on interpersonal relations; he says that seven out of ten people lose their jobs because of personality conflicts.

b.   Are you a likable person?Likable persons possess these qualities: (1) optimism,(2) helpfulness,(3)sense of humor,and (4)self-control.

c.   "Because of your enthusiasm and encouragement,"said Mrs.Steeples,"we were successful.Your assistance was greatly appreciated!"

d.   "The gymnastics class will be held—even if only six people enroll —each Monday and Wednesday,"Liz said.

e.   The policy clearly states: " All employees must arrive promptly at 8: 00 a. m. "

f.   The price increased by 2 . 5 percent — e. g., from $12 . 50 to $ 12 . 81 .

g.   Ms. Gibbs has earned three degrees — a B. S. , an M. B. A. , and a Ph. D.

h.   Mr. J.R. Harper is a well - known consultant.

i.   Three trains arrive at 6 : 15 p. m. (See the enclosed schedule).

j.   In January, costs increased by 3 . 5 percent ; in February, by 4 . 5 percent (see Table 6) .

SECTION P

Capitalization

Capital letters have two main functions: (1) to mark the beginning of a sentence and (2) to mark proper names. Using capital letters makes messages easier to read and to interpret.

PERSONS, TITLES, AND ACADEMIC DEGREES

1. Capitalize people's names exactly as they do.

> Michele D. Moore
> Monica M. de Lipari
> Edward Ray Gorman III
> Bryan A. Stone, Jr.
> R. H. Kasarek

2. Capitalize titles that do the following:
   a. Precede a name

   > They said that President Collins will attend.
   > John Collins, our president, will attend.

   b. Appear in an envelope address, an inside address, or a signature block

   > Dr. Donnie K. Lauer
   > Professor of Economics
   > Lawrence College
   > Morris, AL   35116

   Except in official documents, titles used after a person's name or in place of a name are not capitalized (e.g., Don Smith, sales manager).

   As a mark of respect, however, titles of highest ranking officials in a nation, state, or church are often capitalized even when they follow the name or are used in place of the name. In legal and other official documents, the titles of officers of any organization are often capitalized whenever they are used.

   Ronald Reagan became President of the United States in 1981.
   As President, he has overcome many obstacles.
   The President will visit New Orleans next Tuesday.

3. Capitalize the names of academic degrees and their abbreviations when used with the names of a person. Use the title *Doctor* or *Dr.* before a name only if you are not including the initials of the degree (e.g., M.D., D.B.A., Ph.D., Ed.D.) after the name.

Jody M. March, Ph.D.	Mava T. Hall, M.D. *or*
Miss Maxine D. Herder, CPA	Dr. Mava T. Hall

GEOGRAPHICAL FEATURES, PLACES, ORGANIZATIONS, ASTRONOMICAL BODIES, AND CERTAIN OBJECTS

Use the rules on pages 100-101 for geographical features, places, organizations, astronomical bodies, and certain objects.

1. Capitalize the proper names of geographic areas and features. Included are names of continents, islands, oceans, lakes, rivers, and recognized areas of the world (e.g., *the Mideast*) or of the United States (e.g., *the South*).

   the Atlantic Ocean   Aleutian Islands
   the Colorado River   the Gulf of Alaska
   Lake Erie   Delaware Bay

   Do not capitalize words referring vaguely to an area unless they are part of a proper name. Except in proper names, do not capitalize compass points used to indicate direction.

   west Texas
   University of Northern Colorado
   northern Michigan
   Drive west on I-30 to Fort Worth.

2. Capitalize the proper names and abbreviations of political units, such as communities, towns, cities, counties, states, nations, alliances, and international organizations.

   Hogan County
   Raleigh *or* the city of Raleigh
   Idaho *or* the state of Idaho
   the Bay Area (San Francisco)
   The British Commonwealth
   Big Sky Country
   the United Nations

   Capitalize a common noun such as *city* or *county* when it follows and is a recognized part of a name. Ordinarily, do not capitalize such words if they precede the proper name of the unit or if they are used to replace the proper name.

   Salt Lake City
   the city of San Diego *or* the city
   Kansas City
   the state of Nevada *or* the state

   In legal and other official documents, capitalize such words even when they come before the proper name or when they are used to replace the proper name.

   the City of Philadelphia *or* the City
   the State of Maryland *or* the State

3. Capitalize the proper names of works of civil engineering, such as the names of buildings, bridges, centers, airports, railway depots, dams, streets, tunnels, and monuments.

the Plaza Hotel
the Washington Monument
Buchanan Dam
O'Hare International Airport
Alamosa Drive

Capitalize words such as *street* and *building* when they are a recognized part of a proper name. Except in legal and other official documents, do not capitalize such words when they are used in place of a proper name (e.g., *the building* as a substitute for the *Empire State Building*).

4. Capitalize the proper names of institutions, such as the names of corporations, government units at all levels, schools, foundations, museums, clubs, and charities. Capitalize the names of the major departments and divisions of such organizations.

Capitalize *the* only when it is part of the official name of the organization. Except in legal or other official documents, do not capitalize words such as *company* or *corporation* when they stand alone as a substitute for the entire proper name.

the Mobil Oil Corporation (the company)
the General Accounting Office
The University of Texas (the University)

5. Capitalize the names of stars, planets, and constellations. However, capitalize the nouns *earth*, *sun*, and *moon* only in association with other capitalized astronomical names.

the diameter of the moon
the planets Mars and Earth
the Big Dipper
The moon orbits the earth.

6. Capitalize the proper name of a space shuttle, airplane, ship, or train. Capitalize the manufacturer and proper name of products. Do not capitalize a common noun applying to a product.

the space shuttle *Challenger*
Ford Taurus *but* Ford automobile
Post's Raisin Bran *but* Post's breakfast food

CHECK YOUR UNDERSTANDING 64

Rewrite the following sentences, and use capital letters appropriately:

1. two organizations that help develop leaders are future business leaders of American (fbla) and phi beta lambda (pbl).

2. the three cities that will host the future conventions are denver, colorado; chicago, illinois; and reno, nevada.
3. dr. j. t. cord, jr., lives in the city of san angelo, which is in texas on the concho river.
4. last year, maureen and ed took us to see the grand canyon.
5. at northpark mall, you can purchase clothes at stores such as j. c. penney, dillards, lord and taylor, woolf brothers, and nieman marcus.

CALENDAR TERMS, HOLIDAYS, HISTORICAL PERIODS AND EVENTS

Follow these capitalization rules for calendar terms, holidays, and historical periods and events:

1. Capitalize the names of days of the week and months of the year. Do not capitalize the names of the seasons.

    The temperatures were extremely high in June, July, and August.
    Our managers meet on the third Tuesday of each month.
    My favorite seasons are spring and fall.

2. Capitalize the names of special days.

Passover	Father's Day
Memorial Day	St. Patrick's Day
Christmas	Presidents' Day

3. Capitalize the names of historical periods and important events. Do not capitalize references to centuries. Use figures in referring to decades.

World War I	during the 1980s
the Ice Age	the twentieth century
the Reformation	the Westward Movement

DOCUMENTS, TREATIES, AND PUBLISHED MATERIALS

Follow these capitalization rules for documents, treaties, and published materials:

1. Capitalize the first and all important words in the titles of charters, treaties, declarations, and other official documents.

    Except in legal and other official statements, do not capitalize nouns such as *treaty* or *charter* when used to replace the proper name of the document.

As the first word in the title of a document, capitalize *the* when you use the title as a heading. However, when you use the title within a sentence, do not capitalize *the*.

The U.S. Constitution
but . . . in the U.S. Constitution
The Twelfth Amendment to the United States Constitution
. . . .

2. Capitalize the first word and all important words in the titles of written works. Included are the titles of books, sets of books, reports, studies, journals, magazines, and newspapers. Also, capitalize the first and important words in the titles or headings of sections, divisions, chapters, articles, or other parts of these publications.

World Book Encyclopedia
Chapter 4, "Childhood Diseases," in *The Medical Digest*
Division 3, "Formatting," in *A Guideline for Documents*
Section 7, "Steps to Making a Profit" in *Investing Seriously*

OTHER USES OF CAPITALS

Follow these other capitalization rules:

1. Capitalize the first word of every sentence.

   The desire to excel often produces excellent employees. Recognition and success often follow.

2. Capitalize the first word and all titles and nouns in the salutation of a letter. Capitalize the first word in the complimentary close of a letter.

   Dear Miss Martinez
   Sincerely,
   Ladies and Gentlemen:
   Sincerely yours,
   Dear Dr. Hale
   Very truly yours,

3. Capitalize the pronoun *I* whenever it occurs.

   It was I who edited the booklet for the group.
   In the evening, I enjoy walking with our neighbors.
   When I complete the evaluation process, I will show you the results.

4. Capitalize words referring to the Deity.

  God   the Creator   the Supreme Being

5. Capitalize the names of specific courses of study and the names of languages. However, do not capitalize the names of general fields of study.

   Mr. Norr plans to major in business and English. He is now enrolled in Business 102 and English 201.
   Miss Munsow is studying science courses this quarter; in fact, she just completed a test in Biology 211.

6. Capitalize the first word of a direct quotation when the quoted material is a sentence.

   The manager quickly replied, "Bring your questions to the conference tomorrow."
   The district attorney made the statement: "After all the evidence is presented, we expect to win this case."

7. Capitalize the first word of an independent clause following a colon if you wish to emphasize that clause.

   Mrs. Nicholl's belief was strong: You can become whatever you want to be.

8. Capitalize a noun or abbreviation designating the parts of a written work or designating a chart, a graph, or a diagram when such a designation precedes a number. When these words are not followed by a number, do not capitalize them.

   Volume IX or Vol. IX
   This article is well written.
   Chapter 7 or Chap. 7
   That chapter was interesting.
   Article XVI or Art. XVI

   Except at the beginning of a sentence, do not capitalize these words or their abbreviations: *page/pages, footnote/footnotes,* and *line/lines.*

   Check footnote 10, page 22.
   The references occur on pages 110 through 112 and in lines 1 through 7 of page 114.
   See pp. 35-38, and fn. 16 on p. 34.

9. Capitalize both letters in two-letter state abbreviations.

   OK (Oklahoma)
   OR (Oregon)
   KY (Kentucky)

CHECK YOUR UNDERSTANDING 65

Rewrite the following sentences, and use capital letters appropriately:

1. the chapter "money" of joseph v. smith's book *economics* presents numerous ideas about investing.
2. roberto hernandez and company notified its employees that the office would be closed on friday and monday for christmas.
3. last fall, mr. dennis p. shurr took a math course (algebra 201) at salina state university.
4. the information about the ice age is in chapter 3 on pages 38 through 42.

 EDITING APPLICATIONS

1. Revise the following sentences, using capital letters appropriately:

   a. don m. carter III supported governor reed in his re-election campaign.
   b. This semester, Helen is taking courses in english, math, and psychology; last semester, she studied the westward movement in history 101.
   c. gene gregory, our sales manager, presented numerous awards to the staff at the dallas conference.
   d. ted kesler, a member of the hackberry creek chamber of commerce, will be the announcer.
   e. dr. jerry briscoe has accepted a position with cleary, penn, and company, which has its offices in the haber building in seattle, washington.
   f. the golden gate bridge is a sight many people want to see when they visit san francisco.
   g. our trip to colorado city was on united airlines flight 212.
   h. read unit 1, "getting to know your equipment," in *fast and efficient word processing*.
   i. my mother enjoys her dishwasher; are you pleased with your new dishwasher, evelyn?
   j. mrs. amy hilbert was appointed principal of elton f. carroll high school in rapid city, south dakota.
   k. president marilyn zarco from lane college (located in minneapolis) gave an informative and motivating speech.

l. ms. anita worton, president of wright construction company, announced that the firm had received a large contract and that edmond krynski would be the project manager.

m. on october 10, dr. elizabeth atwood will fly to atlanta, georgia; she plans to leave will rogers international airport, which serves oklahoma city, at 9:00 a.m.

n. you have an interview with president david tabor of lawson, lawson, and douglas inc. at 2:00 p.m. on wednesday, june 3.

o. The joneses plan to vacation on the west coast this summer and go sailing on the pacific ocean on the fourth of july.

p. The shipment will leave birmingham, alabama, by 11:30 a.m., august 15, for the museum of science and industry in chicago, illinois.

q. Send a copy of report no. 12, *safety precautions in storing dangerous chemicals*, to mr. fred tilmon, 422 east vanderbilt road, nashville, tn 37202-4168.

r. in completing an application for a position with starky and company, inc., you must write a brief statement entitled "my employment goals."

s. their consultant is a. j. carmichael, cpa.

t. the internal revenue service has offices in the large cities of every state.

SECTION Q

Expression of Numbers

In business documents such as budgets, payrolls, invoices, purchase orders, and technical reports, use figures to express numbers. However, in messages such as letters, memorandums, and reports, use figures for some numbers and words for others. The following rules will enable you to use words and figures appropriately.

GENERAL GUIDELINES

Follow these general guidelines for expression of numbers:

1. Use words for whole numbers from one through ten.

> The secretary mailed eight copies of the article today.
> Sales have been good; we sold six cars in one day.

Large round numbers are often written in a combination of figures and words.

14 million citizens $3.6 billion

2. Use figures for numbers greater than ten.

The West Side Neighborhood Association reported that 110 people attended the organizational meeting and 87 people attended the crime prevention program.
The 50th person to register will win a prize at the picnic.
We mailed the order for 35 Model 551 computer tables and 75 Model 40 chairs on June 2.

3. Use words for numbers that occur at the beginning of a sentence, as well as any related numbers. Use figures for large numbers and words for numbers ten and under if you use the numbers in different ways in the sentence.

In the last five months, we have driven over 15,000 miles.
Twenty-seven people voted *yes*, and 12 people voted *no*.
Eleven team members paid $54.95 for those shoes, but 12 members paid only $50.95 at another store.
Thirty to forty people will attend the meeting.
Twelve, not fourteen, computers were delivered.

Sometimes it's better to revise a sentence so that the number does not come first.

The results indicated that 27 people voted *yes*, and 12 people voted *no*.
Although 11 team members paid $54.95 for those shoes, 12 members paid only $50.95 at another store.

4. Except at the beginning of a sentence, use figures for all numbers used similarly (including those ten and under) if you use figures for any of the numbers.

The order included 12 reams of paper, 8 printer ribbons, and 6 boxes of labels.
The president mentioned that Abe Jackson had been employed with the company for 18 years; Berna Knox, for 24 years; and Dwight Lankston, for 5 years.

5. If two or more unrelated numbers expressed in figures occur in succession, place a comma between the figures to reduce the danger of confusion.

In 1990, 91 new employees were hired by Sloan, Howell, and Co.
By the end of 1998, 7,000 new homes and businesses will be located in this development.

6. Use figures for the larger of two numbers that occurs in succession; if the smaller number requires more than two words, use figures for both.

Some college students buy twelve 90-cent spiral notebooks at a time.
The employee stamped the company name on 125 230-pound stacks of lumber.

CHECK YOUR UNDERSTANDING 66

Rewrite the following sentences and express all numbers appropriately:

1. Although 8 couples toured the museum with a guide, 6 couples decided to tour without a guide.
2. 20 women registered for the nutrition seminar but only 17 attended.
3. By 1999, 26 hundred students will be attending Lee High School.
4. Lamply has twenty-five thousand citizens, nine hundred ninety-four of whom moved to the city in the last 2 years.

DATES AND TIMES

Follow these rules for expressing dates and times:

1. Use figures expressing cardinal numbers (e.g., 3, 4) for dates.

    Please send the shipment by February 15.
    Mrs. Kruger began her duties as director on October 4.

2. Use ordinal numbers (e.g., third or 3rd) if you refer to the day without referring to the month and year or if you give the month in a prepositional phrase. Figures usually designate emphasis and words designate formality.

    The 2nd of May is the best date for me.
    We will leave for Canada on the 16th.
    You are invited to a reception on the twenty-sixth of November to honor Senator McLaughlin.

3. Use words expressing ordinal numbers for references to centuries. Use figures expressing cardinal numbers (e.g., the 1990s) for decades. However, if you omit the word *century*, use words (e.g., the nineties).

Product design will be extremely different in the twenty-first century.

Many people select the 1950s as a party theme.

In the nineties, it will be even more important to have pollution-free automobile engines.

4. Use figures for times, separate hours from minutes by a colon, and use the abbreviations a.m. (for before midday), m. (for midday), and p.m. (for after midday).

Will Monday, April 12, at 1:30 p.m. be convenient for the nonverbal communication presentation?

The only time available for the teleconference is at 12:00 m. on Friday.

The store is open from 8:00 a.m. until 5:30 p.m.

In formal messages, times are usually given in words followed by the phrase *o'clock*.

The pleasure of your company is requested at a reception to be held on the sixteenth of January at two o'clock in the Oak Room of the Dumont Hotel.

We will meet at seven o'clock in the Jefferson Room.

ADDRESSES

Follow these rules for expressing addresses:

1. Use figures for house numbers except *one*.

5135 East Monroe Street
4 North Maple Circle
One Dove Circle

2. Use figures or words for numbered streets as practiced by the particular city. Cities often use words for streets numbered one through ten and figures for streets numbered eleven and above. Many cities use the letters *st, nd, rd, d,* and *th* after figures in street names over ten.

If the words *east, west, south,* or *north* are not part of the street name, use a hyphen (preceded and followed by a space) between the house number and street number to make the address easier to read.

127 Third Avenue
824 - 75th Avenue
328 West 16 Street
642 - 53rd Street
177 - 63 Street

3. Use figures for numbered highways.

Interstate 35   Illinois Route 40   U.S. Route 66

AMOUNTS OF MONEY

Follow these rules for expressing amounts of money:

1. In letters, memorandums, and other informal messages, use figures for sums of money. For even sums, omit the decimal and zeros unless other sums in the same context include decimal fractions.

> Remember to add $28.74 for taxes.
> The new car will cost $19,464.
> The three dresses cost $40.00, $45.00, and $55.98.

2. On checks, write sums in figures, and repeat them in words to confirm the amount. In contracts and other legal documents, write sums in words. For confirmation, repeat them in figures within parentheses. (In writing sums in words, use *and* only to represent a decimal point. In such contexts, use fractions or decimal fractions to indicate cents. Capitalization is optional but preferred.)

I agree to pay Nancy Aldaco the sum of Five Thousand Two Hundred Eighty-four and $^{37}/_{100}$ Dollars ($5,284.37) on or before July 18.
The charge for these services will be Twenty-one Thousand One Hundred Sixty-seven and $^{00}/_{100}$ Dollars ($21,167.00).

3. Use a combination of figures and words (preceded by $) for large approximate amounts.

The budget for next year is $15.1 million.

4. Use figures and the word *cents* for amounts less than one dollar. However, use $.64 in a sentence that has related amounts that require dollar signs.

> 64 cents
> Those items cost $2.74, $1.25, and $.37, respectively.

CHECK YOUR UNDERSTANDING 67

Rewrite the following sentences, and express numbers appropriately:

1. The address of Mrs. Vernell Ade, our newest client, is Thirty-three Forty-nine 5th Street. Her office address is 1 West One Hundred and Seventy-seventh Street.

2. When you reach the intersection of Walnut Hill Lane and Interstate Thirty-five E, turn south on Interstate Thirty-five E and continue to downtown Dallas.
3. For the training program on October 16th, please bring your company manual.
4. The land for the proposed shopping mall will cost at least 30,000,000 dollars.
5. The Presidents' Reception will be in the Imperial Ballroom from six to eight p.m.
6. One costs two dollars and twenty-five cents, and the other costs seventy-five cents.

FRACTIONS, DECIMALS, AND PERCENTAGES

Follow these rules for expressing fractions, decimals, and percentages:

1. Use words for simple fractions and place a hyphen between the parts of a fraction.

   Mr. Aaron discovered that two-thirds of his class had already studied statistics.
   They spent three-fourths of their monthly income paying bills.
   A two-thirds majority is needed to approve an amendment.

2. Use figures for mixed fractions and decimal fractions. To confirm the correctness of a decimal fraction not preceded by a whole number, use a zero before the decimal point.

   The size of the room is 12 ½ feet by 13 ¾ feet.
   The size of the room is 12.5 feet by 13.75 feet.
   I used 0.038 for the calculation.

3. Use figures followed by the word *percent* for percents.

   The interest rate fluctuates; today it is 8 percent.
   Miss Terri Acree still owes 25 percent of the principal.

QUANTITIES AND MEASUREMENTS

Follow these rules for expressing quantities and measurements:

1. Use figures for dimensions, weights, and distances. Except in technical writing, use *by* rather than *x* between numbers expressing dimensions.

   7 inches by 10 ¼ inches
   458 miles
   36 pounds

Customarily, use words for fractions when the fraction is followed by an *of* phrase.

The store is only nine-tenths of a mile from home.

2. Use figures followed by the degree sign (or the word *degrees*) and the name or abbreviation of the scale involved.

It feels as if it is about 10° C or 50° F.
We nearly froze during the meeting because the temperature was 60 degrees Fahrenheit.

3. Use words to indicate approximate ages and time periods. Use figures when greater accuracy is necessary (e.g., for statistics or technical measurements).

Susan is twenty-one years old.
The minimum age requirement for this position is 21.
The average life expectancy for that group is 78 years and 7 months.

WRITTEN MATERIALS

Follow these rules for numbering written materials:

1. Number the pages of any piece of writing more than one page long with figures.

2. Use Arabic numerals for pages in the main part of a work; use small Roman numerals (i.e., *ii, iv*) in a preface or introduction.

OFFICIAL NAMES AND DESIGNATIONS

Use figures or words as practiced by the organization involved.

112th Precinct   First Methodist Church   Ninth Naval District

CHECK YOUR UNDERSTANDING 68

Rewrite the following sentences, and express numbers appropriately:

1. The storage space is five and one-half feet by seven and one-half feet.
2. A sample spreadsheet is shown on page five of Volume Two of the computer manual.
3. Mr. Thompson needs the report by 10:30 a.m. o'clock on Wednesday, February 12th.

4. Students will receive a fifteen percent discount if they purchase the sports clothes by Thursday, June fifth.
5. Mr. Lake said they will use ½ of the profits for new band uniforms.

EDITING APPLICATIONS

1. Revise the following sentences, expressing numbers appropriately:

   a. Chart No. Three on page six summarizes the survey data.
   b. The seven and one-half percent sales tax increased the cost by Four Dollars and eighty-three cents.
   c. Our firm now has twelve partners and eight secretaries.
   d. Debra decided that seventy-five ten-cent plants would complete the garden.
   e. The population has increased to approximately one point five million people.
   f. In 1990, five hundred sixty two new houses were built in the new Aztec Hill development.
   g. You are invited to attend our grand opening at one hundred thirty-three South 8th Street on August 15th at ten a.m.
   h. How can you sell those kitchen utensils for only $.88 each?
   i. The voters supported three fourths of the amendments.
   j. On July 22nd, the board of city planners will meet at 12 for lunch and a meeting.
   k. During the nineteen eighties, loud rock music caused hearing losses.
   l. The box measured five inches by seven inches.
   m. Please deliver the brass lamps to Kim Osuga's home at 1 Hampton Way by Tuesday, September 12th.
   n. The calf gained one hundred and six pounds in five months.
   o. We estimate that thirty-five% of our staff will attend the conference.
   p. The test had seventy-five questions.
   q. Please respond by the 23 of June.
   r. 15 of the doctors had been on the staff for more than 10 years.
   s. The tour guide said that ½ of the group would stay at the Hotel Pierre.
   t. The graduation ceremony will begin at 2 p.m.
   u. When I picked up the order, I had seven trophies, 15 plaques, and 22 ribbons.
   v. Mr. Lee will be out of the office for three and one-half days next week.

   w. Deliver the twelve packages to ten West 15th Street.

   x. The expected cost of the expansion is 1.3 million dollars.

   y. 230 teachers attended the workshop on May 2nd.

   z. In the last 3 hours, we have registered 75 runners for the 10-mile race on Saturday.

  aa. We will divide the computer seminar into 3 2-hour sessions.

  bb. Susan will publish 4 articles on letter writing in the November 28th issue of *Writing Styles*.

  cc. The Special Olympics will be held from 8 a.m. until 730 p.m. on Friday.

  dd. The price of the computer has decreased one hundred and twenty five dollars during the last six months.

  ee. The contract states: "Allen E. Pearson agrees to pay Grace R. Appleton Ten Thousand Two Hundred and Twelve and $^{25}/_{100}$ Dollars for Lot No. eight."

   ff. During the sale Lampley's reduced the prices on sixty items by 20 to 30%.

  gg. Before the bylaws can be changed, $\frac{2}{3}$ of the members present must vote in favor of the amendments.

  hh. Ellen said that the orange juice costs 75¢.

   ii. Standard stationery measures eight inches and one half by eleven inches.

SECTION R

Spelling

Effective messages have correctly spelled words.

There is one correct way to spell a word but many ways to misspell a word. That is why improving your spelling requires concentration and conscientious practice. This section presents methods for improving your spelling.

WRITING INDIVIDUAL WORDS

To improve your spelling, use a dictionary. Write difficult words correctly in longhand. Write them many times. Write such words repeatedly as many days in succession as necessary to learn their spelling.

KINDS OF MISSPELLINGS

To improve your spelling, begin by identifying the kinds of misspellings you make. Then use Table R-1 to determine tactics to correct those types of misspellings. Some of the tactics involve spelling rules which are presented on pages 116-121.

TABLE R-1   KINDS OF MISSPELLINGS

Error	Tactic for Improvement
1. Getting *ie* and *ei* in the wrong order	Learn and apply Rule 1 (page 116).
2. Not doubling final consonants appropriately	Learn and apply Rule 2 (page 116).
3. Not changing final *y* to *i* appropriately	Learn and apply Rule 3 (page 118).
4. Not handling final *e* appropriately before endings	Learn and apply Rule 4 (page 120).
5. Mispronunciations (often involve reversing the order of certain letters or inserting an extra syllable)	Learn to pronounce these words correctly (page 124).
6. Writing one word when you mean a different word	Become familiar with the sound-alike words that confuse you (page 127).
7. Personal misspellings belonging to none of the previous categories	Create memory devices to help you with troublesome words (page 127).
8. Lack of familiarity with frequently misspelled words likely to occur in messages	Learn to spell the words on the master lists (pages 130-134).

CHECK YOUR UNDERSTANDING 69

Spell the following words correctly, and write the appropriate tactic for learning to avoid each misspelling:

reciept   attornies   industrys   nineth   acknowledgement
regreted   incidently   carful   seperate   stationary (paper)

SPELLING RULES

Learn these four rules to improve your spelling.

Rule 1. The Order of ie and ei

Write *i* before *e* except after *c* or when sounded like *a* as in *neighbor* and *weigh*.

The words covered by this rule and the words that are exceptions to it are among the most frequently misspelled words.

IE	EI after C	EI Sounded like A	Exceptions
achieve	conceive	eight	either
believe	deceit	eighth	financier
belief	deceive	freight	foreign*
brief	perceive	neighbor	height*
chief	receipt	weigh	leisure
field	receive	weight	neither
friend			seize
mischief			their*
piece			
relief			
relieve			

*Note: The *ei* spelling in these words does *not* represent the *ee* sound.

CHECK YOUR UNDERSTANDING 70

From the lists above, have someone dictate seven words at random that follow the rule and three words at random that are exceptions. Try to spell them correctly. Continue with the same group of words until you spell them all correctly.

Repeat the above procedure using different words.

Rule 2. Doubling Final Consonants

If one-syllable words (or two-syllable words accented on the second syllable) are spelled with single vowels (i.e., *a, e, i, o,* or *u*) and end in a single consonant (i.e., a letter other than those listed before), double the final consonant before adding an ending beginning with a vowel.

This rule applies to the *-ing* and *-ed* forms of many verbs and to many other words that add endings like *-ence* or *-able*.

Base Word	-ed Added	-ing Added	Other Endings Added
ban	banned	banning	
begin		beginning	beginner
commit	committed	committing	committee
compel	compelled	compelling	
confer	conferred	conferring	
control	controlled	controlling	
defer	deferred	deferring	
equip	equipped	equipping	
fan	fanned	fanning	
fit	fitted	fitting	
forget		forgetting	
get		getting	
hit		hitting	hitter
let		letting	
occur	occurred	occurring	occurrence
omit	omitted	omitting	
permit	permitted	permitting	
plan	planned	planning	planner
prefer	preferred	preferring	
propel	propelled	propelling	propeller
red			redder/reddest
refer	referred	referring	
regret	regretted	regretting	regrettable
remit	remitted	remitting	remittance
repel	repelled	repelling	repellent
run		running	runner
sad			sadder/saddest
sit		sitting	sitter
stop	stopped	stopping	
transfer	transferred	transferring	
transmit	transmitted	transmitting	
wed	wedded	wedding	
wet	wetted	wetting	wetter/wettest

CHECK YOUR UNDERSTANDING 71

Have someone dictate the following list of verbs. Write the past tense and the -ing form of each verb. Repeat this activity until you spell all the words correctly.

transfer	drop	occur	confer	plan
remit	control	equip	step	infer

| commit | benefit | permit | omit | submit |
| offer | regret | refer | prefer | defer |

Rule 3.   Changing *Y* to *I*

Change a final *y* preceded by a consonant to *i* before adding any ending except *-ing*.

This rule covers many noun plurals, many verb forms, and other parts of speech that end in *y* and add endings.

Singular Noun	Plural Noun
activity	activities
baby	babies
candy	candies
capacity	capacities
city	cities
company	companies
county	counties
country	countries
currency	currencies
democracy	democracies
facility	facilities
enemy	enemies
industry	industries
lady	ladies
salary	salaries
secretary	secretaries
study	studies
supply	supplies
university	universities

Base Verb	Third-Person Singular	Past Tense	*-ing* Added
apply	applies	applied	applying
accompany	accompanies	accompanied	accompanying
carry	carries	carried	carrying
comply	complies	complied	complying
cry	cries	cried	crying
defy	defies	defied	defying
fortify	fortifies	fortified	fortifying
imply	implies	implied	implying

marry	marries	married	marrying
rely	relies	relied	relying
reply	replies	replied	replying
study	studies	studied	studying
supply	supplies	supplied	supplying
testify	testifies	testified	testifying
try	tries	tried	trying
vary	varies	varied	varying

Positive Adjective/Adverb	Comparative Adjective/Adverb	Superlative Adjective/Adverb
busy	busier	busiest
dry	drier	driest
early	earlier	earliest
easy	easier	easiest
friendly	friendlier	friendliest
happy	happier	happiest
lively	livelier	liveliest
lonely	lonelier	loneliest
silly	sillier	silliest
sleepy	sleepier	sleepiest
wary	warier	wariest
weary	wearier	weariest

Base Word	-ly Added	-ness Added	-ous Added
busy	busily	business	
crafty	craftily	craftiness	
easy	easily	easiness	
friend	friendly	friendliness	
happy	happily	happiness	
hazy	hazily	haziness	
heavy	heavily	heaviness	
industry			industrious
lazy	lazily	laziness	
live	lively	liveliness	
lone	lonely	loneliness	
silly		silliness	
sleepy	sleepily	sleepiness	
steady	steadily	steadiness	
study			studious
sturdy	sturdily	sturdiness	
vary			various

Have someone dictate the following lists of verbs and nouns. Write the third-person singular present tense form of the verbs and the plural form of the nouns. Repeat this activity until you can spell all the words correctly.

Verbs	Nouns
study	city
apply	secretary
reply	lady
comply	industry
supply	activity
accompany	county
imply	facility

Rule 4. Keeping or Omitting Final *E* When Adding an Ending

Keep a silent final *e* before adding an ending beginning with a *consonant*. Usually omit a silent final *e* before adding an ending beginning with a *vowel*.

Words Ending in Silent *E*	With Endings Beginning with a Consonant (*E* Retained)	With Endings Beginning with a Vowel (*E* Dropped)
achieve	achievement	achieving
argue		arguing
arrange	arrangement	arranging
base	basement	basing
become		becoming
believe		believable/believing
change		changing
care	careful	caring
come		coming
complete	completeness	completing/completion
conceive		conceivable/conceiving
crude	crudeness	crudity
cure		curable/curing

decide	decidedly	deciding
desire		desirable/desiring
endure		enduring/endurance
entire	entirely/entirety	
encourage	encouragement	encouraging
evaluate		evaluating/evaluation
excite	excitedly/excitement	excitable/exciting
fame		famous
lone	lonely	
lose		losing
manage	management	managing
practice		practical/practicing
receive		receivable/receiver/receiving
retire	retirement	retiring
rude	rudeness	
separate	separately/separateness	separation
severe	severely	severity
sincere	sincerely	sincerity
use	useful	using

EXCEPTIONS TO THE RULES FOR FINAL *E*

Sometimes the final *e* is dropped with an ending beginning with a consonant.

acknowledge	acknowledgment
argue	argument
awe	awful
judge	judgment
nine	ninth
true	truly
wide	width
wise	wisdom

Sometimes the final *e* is retained with an ending beginning with a vowel.

change	changeable
courage*	courageous
knowledge*	knowledgeable

                notice*   noticeable
                manage*   manageable

    *Note: The *e* retained in these words indicates the sound of the preceding consonant.

CHECK YOUR UNDERSTANDING 73

Have someone dictate each of the following words and the ending given after the words. Spell the word with the ending given. Proceed in this way through the list of words. Repeat this activity until you can spell all the words correctly.

Word	Ending	Word	Ending
necessary	ly	nine	ty
achieve	ment	entire	ly
receive	able	lose	ing
excite	ment	desire	able
notice	able	argue	ment
complete	ing	knowledge	able

 EDITING APPLICATIONS

1. Revise the following sentences, spelling all words correctly. Indicate which spelling rule applies to any misspelling you find.

    a. Your letter requested that we deliver the supplys to your office.

    b. The management center staff easly completed the project.

    c. Many company employees have questions about their group insureance rates.

    d. The consultants received further encouragment when the workshop was evaluated; the participants said the experience was valueable.

    e. Our school requires complyance with those regulations.

    f. Staff members may receive continueing education credit.

    g. The printer mistakenly omited the paragraph about savings plans.

    h. The attornies implyed that the contract was unsatisfactory.

    i. Mrs. Raney's claim was refered to the appropriate committee.

    j. Last night the air conditioner made a wierd noise.

    k. The board is considering permiting the commitie two months to complete that project.

l.   We are baseing our forecast on recent computer orders.
m.   Please send an acknowledgement by April 22.
n.   The response to the training sessions has steadyly improved.
o.   Did you obtain a reciept for the delivery?
p.   Our director's performance evalueation is scheduled on Wednes-day.
q.   During that period, Mrs. Helms controled the research funds.
r.   Additional insurance coverage is extremly important for valueable jewelry.
s.   Before begining on the project, the director talked to approximatly eight people.
t.   Miss Day is the most knowledgeable manager in the firm.

2.   In each of the following lines, select the correct spelling of the word:

a.	beleive	beleeve	believe
b.	prefering	preferring	prefirring
c.	facilityes	facilitys	facilities
d.	livelier	livelyer	livelyier
e.	secretarys	secretaries	secretaryies
f.	argueing	arguying	arguing
g.	receiveable	receivable	receevable
h.	acknowledgment	acknowlegement	aknowledgment
i.	ocurred	occured	occurred
j.	frate	freight	frieght
k.	accomodate	acommodate	accommodate
l.	curencies	currencies	curencys
m.	accompanying	accompaning	acompanying
n.	friendlyest	freindliest	friendliest
o.	replys	replies	replis
p.	acheeving	acheiving	achieving
q.	manageble	manageable	managable
r.	weigh	wiegh	waigh
s.	necessaryly	necessarily	necesarily
t.	separetly	separetely	separately

3.   In each of the following words, add *ie* or *ei*, to correctly spell the word defined:

a.	rel__ve	(ease; reduce)
b.	__ghth	(the number after seventh)
c.	h__ght	(measurement from top to bottom)
d.	financ__r	(person skilled in finance)
e.	bel__ve	(accept as true)
f.	rec__pt	(proof of payment)

g. l__sure   (time free from work)
h. misch__f   (annoying action)
i. th__r   (possessive of *them*)
j. s__ze   (grasp)

SECTION S

Spelling Clues from Pronunciation and Memory Devices

Spelling generally relates to our pronunciation of words. For example, differences in spelling reflect the differences in pronunciation between long and short vowels. Long vowels have the sound of their own name. Short vowels do not.

SPELLING CLUES FOR WORDS WITH LONG VOWELS

Words with long vowels in their accented syllables tend to have the following characteristics:

1. They end in silent *e* (especially true of words with long *a*, long *i*, and long *u*). Do not double consonants when you add endings to these words.

Word with Long *A*	Word with Long *E*	Word with Long *I*	Word with Long *U*	Ending Added
		bite		biter
	cede			ceding
	concede			conceding
			cute	cuter
date				dated
		dine		dining
name				naming
	precede			preceded
			pure	purer
rate				rating
			tube	tubing
		write		writing

2. They require two letters (such as *ie*) to spell their long vowel sound (especially true of long *e*, long *o*, and of the combination sound *ou*). Do not double consonants when you add endings to these words.

Word with Long *E* Sound	Word with Long *O* Sound	Word With Combination *OU* Sound	Ending Added
brief			briefer
	float		floating
meet			meeting
	moan		moaning
		loud	louder
	soap		soapy
		sound	sounding

SPELLING CLUES FOR WORDS WITH SHORT VOWELS

Words with short vowels use a single letter to spell their vowel. Also, such words end with a consonant or sequence of consonants rather than with a silent *e*. If you add an ending that begins with a vowel to such words, *double a single final consonant before you add the ending*.

Word with Short *A*	Word with Short *E*	Word with Short *I*	Word with Short *O*	Word with Short *U*	Ending Added
bat					batted
		bit			bitten
				bud	budding
				cut	cutting
			dot		dotted
fan					fanned
		fit			fitted
			fog		foggy
	get				getting
			mop		mopping
pass					passing
	red				redder
		slip			slipping
				tug	tugged

The clues indicated on page 124 often can be helpful in longer words, too. For example, a common misspelling is *proNOUNciation* for the word *pronunciation* as though the main vowel were the same as in the word *proNOUNce*. If you pronounce the word correctly (i.e., *pro-NUNciation*), the correct spelling of the word will be much easier.

CONSONANT CLUES

You can avoid many misspellings through careful attention to consonant sounds and to the sequence of sounds in words. For example, the mispronunciation *childERn* for *childREn* sometimes leads to a misspelling in which the *r* is placed after rather than before the *e*. Similarly, the mispronunciation *hundERd* for *hundREd* sometimes leads to a reversal of the order of *r* and *e*.

Below is a list of words you should learn to pronounce accurately to help you avoid misspellings. The italicized letters are the part of the word requiring special care.

accompa*ny*ing (five syllables)	la*tt*er
accustome*d* to	leng*t*h
ath*lete* (two syllables)	lib*r*ary
ath*letic*s (three syllables)	main*ten*ance
can*d*idate	particula*r*ly
child*r*en	p*r*edict
envi*r*onment	p*r*efer
eve*r*ybody	p*r*escription
eve*r*yone	p*r*ob*ab*ly (three syllables)
February	pro*nun*ciation
gove*r*nment	quan*t*ity
gove*r*nor	recognize
hind*r*ance (two syllables)	sec*r*etary
hund*r*ed	streng*t*h
interp*r*et	su*r*prise
irre*lev*ant	use*d* to

Other spelling mistakes result from informal, conversational pronunciations rather than from mispronunciations. Thus, the omission or slurring of vowel sounds in unaccented syllables of words sometimes leads to spelling problems. For example, *sophomore* is often pronounced as though it were spelled *sophmore*. *Accidentally* is often pronounced as though it were spelled *accidently*. *Practically* is often pronounced as though it were spelled *practicly*. *Incidentally* is often pronounced as *incidently*.

CHECK YOUR UNDERSTANDING 74

Have someone dictate the words on page 127. As you write the words, pronounce them slowly to yourself. Use your pronunciation of the word as a guide in spelling the word. Repeat this activity until you can spell the words correctly.

accidentally	everybody	interesting	probably
accompanying	everything	irrelevant	quantity
attitude	February	library	strength
candidate	government	particularly	surprise
environment	hindrance	practically	used to

MEMORY DEVICES

When pronunciation is of no help (as when two words sound alike), use memory devices to help you spell the word correctly. Memorize catchy sayings or ideas that remind you of the correct spelling.

The sayings or ideas don't have to be logical. Sometimes memory devices that are outlandish are easiest to remember and most helpful. For example, a frequent misspelling is *doSEn't* for *doESn't*. Many people avoid that mistake by recalling, every time they write this word, that "*Doesn't* never includes a *dose*."

Below are other memory devices for avoiding common misspellings. Use these examples to help with the words involved and to give you suggestions for making up sayings of your own. Memory devices will continue to be helpful as long as you use them regularly.

Word	Memory Device
parallel	Two *ls*; the *ls* within the word are parallel. One *r* is *par* for *parallel*.
principle	When this word means *rule* it ends like ruLE. Use *princiPAL* for all other meanings.
separate	The second syllable of this word is like *aPARt*, which is what the word means.
their	*Their* is the possessive of *they*. Change the *y* to *i* before adding *r*.
recognition	*ReCOGnition* is the *cog* of courtesy.
exceed succeed proceed	Three words end with *ceed*: *exceed*, *succeed*, and *proceed*. Remember the letters *e s p* so that you can recall the words.
supersede	Only one word ends with *sede*: supersede. Remember that this word also begins with an *s*.

CHECK YOUR UNDERSTANDING 75

Invent memory devices for avoiding the following mistakes in spelling:

Misspelling		Correct Spelling
acomodate	for	accommodate
advice	for	advise
assistence	for	assistance
discription	for	description
familar	for	familiar
grammer	for	grammar
loose	for	lose
mispelling	for	misspelling
ocasion	for	occasion
reccomend	for	recommend

DICTIONARY USE

The dictionary is a valuable tool for any communicator. No matter how expert one may be in spelling, anyone who writes much must frequently consult the dictionary or use a computer spell checker to determine correct spellings and word divisions.

When you write, develop the habit of verifying the spelling of difficult and unfamiliar words. Using the dictionary frequently will help you become a better speller.

EDITING APPLICATIONS

1. Revise the following sentences, correcting all misspellings. For each misspelled word, be prepared to state whether the vowel in the accented syllable of the word is long or short. Also, be prepared to explain how the spelling of the word reflects this fact.

    Example: The flag bearer *preceeded* the athletes as they entered the stadium.

    Correction: The flag bearer *preceded* the athletes as they entered the stadium.

    Explanation: The vowel of *precede* is long; precede is not one of the *ceed* words.

    a. Miss Gonzales is writting the summary of the report.
    b. That check was datted incorrectly.

   c. Carla was biten by Mr. Finegan's dog.
   d. The attorneys were hopping that you would agree to the proposal.
   e. The noise of the equipment is mutted by the thick carpeting.
   f. Running in the hallways has been baned.
   g. Mr. Camarillo has copped exceptionally well with the changes.
   h. The work schedules were writen in longhand.
   i. Our firm has been cuting work hours each month.
   j. Mae Stokes was the winer of the bicycle race.

2. Revise the following sentences, correcting all misspellings. For each misspelled word, cite a detail of pronunciation or a memory device that would enable a writer to avoid the mistake.

    Example: The *sophmore* class will sell Christmas cards to raise money.

    Correction: The *sophomore* class will sell Christmas cards to raise money.

    Citation: Pronounce the *o* between *soph* and *more*.

   a. The childern's rooms are being redecorated.
   b. Mispellings in reports and file records create a poor impression.
   c. The faculty secretry is preparing the minutes.
   d. Our customers perfer liberal credit terms and inexpensive merchandise.
   e. Their service policies are similiar to ours.
   f. The principle reason for the rebate is to increase sales.
   g. Our employees paid thier own expenses to attend the seminar.
   h. Are you familar with our quality products?
   i. Mr. and Mrs. Ingram have seperate checking accounts.
   j. We are hiring additional sales personal.
   k. Miss Kahn is particulerly careful about making payments on time.
   l. The cost is approximately 20 percent less if you buy larger quanities of paper.
   m. Many organizations are becoming involved in protecting the enviorment.
   n. Some courses were accidently omitted from the university catalog.
   o. Our school libary is the largest in the district.

3. In each of the following lines, select the correctly spelled word. Then create a memory device for the word.

a.	corparation	corporation	corpration
b.	reguarding	regarding	reguardding
c.	material	materiel	meterial
d.	proceadures	proceedures	procedures

e.	financial	fanancial	finanshial
f.	approximatley	approxamately	approximately
g.	receive	recieve	receeve
h.	dicision	decision	desicion
i.	maintainance	maintenance	maintanence

SECTION T

Master Spelling Lists

This section contains words you should learn to spell before the end of this course. They are words that occur often in messages and that are frequently misspelled.

An excellent system for improving your spelling is to master one ten-word list at a time. When you believe you can spell the words in a particular list, take a written test on those words.

Proceed to the next list only when you have mastered every word in the list you have been working on. In studying each list, apply the four spelling rules whenever you can. (See Section R.) Write the words repeatedly in longhand, and develop memory devices for words that give you special difficulty. When you can spell these words and understand and use the rules applicable to them, you will have made tremendous progress toward being a good speller.

SPELLING LISTS

Master List 1

accurate
business
choose
complete
definitely
entirely
forward
stopping
usually
whose (as in "whose book")

Master List 2

allotment
capital (as in "capital for investment")
distributor
imaginary
interference
lease
personally
remittance
several
your (as in "your opportunity")

Master List 3

acquire
expense
height
ninety
passed (as in "passed by")
safety
studying
therefore
they're (as in "they're here")
where (as in "where are they?")

Master List 4

accuracy
choice
definition
government
maintenance
piece (as in "a piece of cloth")
recommend
salary
straight
utilize

Master List 5

across
bargain
convenience
later
numerous
personnel (as in "office personnel")
possession
recognize
scientists
you're (as in "you're welcome")

Master List 6

applicant
dealer
forty
freight
naturally
noticing
occurrence
operation
separately
service

Master List 7

applies
embarrass
fundamentally
interfere
laid (as in "the carpet was laid")
meant
past (as in "the bill was past due")
receipt
secretary
who's (as in "who's been appointed?")

Master List 8

category
course (as in "a course of action")
encourage
influence
medicine
mortgage
pertain
probably
similar
tendency

Master List 9

acknowledgment
corporation
different
guarantee
hindrance
knowledge
procedure
schedule
studied
wealth

Master List 10

a lot (as in "a lot of
   support")
apparent
applied
carrying
commercial
extremely
losing
policies
principle (as in "a principle
   to follow")
stopped

Master List 11

accept
argument
changing
competitive
due (as in "the bill is due")
especially
indispensable
persuade
separate (as in "separate
   files")
sufficient

Master List 12

all right (as in "It's all right
   with me.")
coming
convenient
encouragement
existence
finally
personal (as in "personal
   opinion")
prepare
resources
their (as in "their work")

Master List 13

accurately
attitude
believe
laboratory
paid
performance
preference
repetition
success
through (as in "through the
   door")

Master List 14

accidentally
completely
divide
equipped
fourth (as in "third, fourth")
opinion
principal (as in "principal
   goal")
relief
than (as in "more than
   enough")
writing

Master List 15

appreciate
customer
decision
equipment
facilitate
occasion
omit
practiced
preferred
referred

Master List 16

becoming
easily
familiar
noticeable
particularly
practical
receive
relevant
there (meaning "in that
    place")
women

Master List 17

accommodate
accountable
benefited
interest
it's (as in "it's ready")
opportunity
parallel
possess
surprise
transferred

Master List 18

amount
effect (as in "the effect of
    inflation")
led (as in "has led the staff")
omitted
planning
pleasant
quantity
source
summary
tomorrow

Master List 19

article
beneficial
commission
efficient
lose (as in "Don't lose a
    minute.")
occurred
preparation
succeed
valuable
write (as in "write a check")

Master List 20

appearance
beginning
bought
doesn't
everything (one word)
hundred
precede (meaning "to go
    before")
seize
thoroughly
unnecessary

Master List 21

appropriate
calendar
committee

Master List 22

career
cashier
certainly

eighth
excellent
foreign
industries
leisure
sincerely
twelfth

guidance
independent
merchandise
priorities
shipper
too (as in "I'll go too.")
wholesale

Master List 23

advertisement
buy (meaning "to purchase")
deliveries
discrepancy
economy
executive
loan (as in "a $5 loan")
retailer
statistical
taxable

Master List 24

competing
concerned
dividend
enclosure
itemize
latter (meaning "second of
    two items")
license
merchandising
percent
royalties

CHECK YOUR UNDERSTANDING 76

Rewrite the following message, correcting all misspellings:

The reciever of a messege will usualy be extremly offended by
finding mispellings. One explenation that is somtimes offerred for
the occurence of such misteaks is that in writting the messege or in
perparing it, everbody hurryed to meat a dedline. The secertarys
were use to having more time. However, if secretaries use this
excuse, they are forgeting thier prioretys. If they believe its more
importent in preforming thier dutys to male a leter promtly then to
male a acurate leter, there serously confussed. Such carlessness is
inexcuseable.

EDITING APPLICATIONS

1. Revise the following sentences, correcting all misspellings:

    a. Mr. Marlow used the same proceedure for the construction of
        this house.

    b. The commission members sincerely appreciated your support.

c. Miss Nye discussed their additudes with them.
d. These organizations have definitly improved their status in the community's image.
e. The new training program is designed for office personal.
f. The students showed thier enthusiasm during the pep rally.
g. Last month's expence accounts are attached.
h. Are you familar with the new policy?
i. The members of the operations department recieved a salary increase.
j. Pearson Insurance Agency is changeing the premium due dates.
k. He doesn't know the amount of Miss Hooper's last lone.
l. Those two ommissions were costly for the division.
m. Most of their distributors have had to wait to months for their sales merchandise.
n. Under the circumstances, Mr. Peyton dosen't believe he should send the check.
o. I have marked the dates for the craft shows on my calender.
p. He finely planted the flowers in a sunny area.
q. Mr. Proctor has payed his April telephone bill.
r. Some interesting data have resulted from these labratory experiments.
s. The buyers will take possesion of the property next Monday.
t. Did Miss Raines chose all the additional furnishings?
u. Miss Tishoto's savings acount has a substantial balance.
v. Mr. Porter was trying to perswade our employees to attend the training program.
w. Will you be able to acommodate all the people who responded?
x. Following the first item on the agenda, we will discuss a summery of the research project.
y. Her dance group siezed the opportunity to participate in the May program.
z. To succede in business, excellent communication skills are essential.
aa. At the special occassion, Miss Cromwell sent congradulatory messages to the staff members who received awards.
bb. Last year, Mr. Burgess sold more word processing software then Mr. Byrum did.
cc. They refered his federal income tax questions to Miss Crowley.
dd. Your morgage payment is due on the 15th of each month.

2. Compose a rule or memory device to help you spell each of the following words correctly:

a.	accommodate	i.	familiar
b.	acknowledgment	j.	occasion
c.	benefited	k.	occurrence
d.	capital	l.	principal
e.	convenience	m.	recommend
f.	definitely	n.	separately
g.	effect	o.	similar
h.	embarrass		

SECTION U

Word Division

Many word processing programs enable an operator to print messages with an even right margin. Similarly, skillful keyboarders can key messages with a relatively even right margin. To achieve this effect, a word processor or keyboarder must divide some words at the ends of lines. In these cases, divide words only between syllables. (When in doubt, use a dictionary.) In addition, follow these guidelines:

1. Do not divide one-syllable words.

rough   leave   print

2. Put enough of the divided word at the end of the first line so that the reader will be able to anticipate what the full word is. Put enough of the word on the following line so that it seems sensible to divide the word.

photog-rapher not pho-tographer
not photogra-pher

Leave at least two letters of the word at the end of the first line and place at least three letters or two letters and a punctuation mark on the next line. Otherwise, place the entire word on one line or the other.

amaz-ing not a-mazing
bio-graphic not biograph-ic

3.   Avoid dividing words with five or fewer letters.

order *not* or-der
after *not* af-ter
final *not* fi-nal

Also, try to avoid dividing words of six letters.

margin *not* mar-gin
letter *not* let-ter
divide *not* di-vide

4.   Do not divide an expression involving a contraction.

wasn't *not* was-n't
couldn't *not* could-n't

5.   If you doubled a consonant to add an ending, divide the word between the doubled consonants.

omit-ted *not* omitt-ed
forgot-ten *not* forgott-en
split-ting *not* splitt-ing

However, if a word already ends in a double consonant before you add an ending, divide the word between the last consonant and the ending.

fall-ing *not* fal-ling
tell-ing *not* tel-ling

CHECK YOUR UNDERSTANDING 77

Rewrite the following words. Insert a hyphen at each proper dividing point, if any, for these words. Write *no* after words that you should not divide.

swimming	hadn't	objecting	agreement
broken	possessing	enjoy	please

---

6.   Include with the first part of a divided word a single-letter syllable within the word.

organi-zation *not* organ-ization
compara-tive *not* compar-ative

When two one-letter syllables occur together within a word, divide the word between those syllables.

gradu-ation *not* gradua-tion
pronunci-ation *not* pronuncia-tion

When *-ble*, *-bly*, *-cle*, or *-cal* is the final syllable and is preceded by a syllable consisting of a single vowel, include the vowel with the second part of the word. (This rule does not apply unless the vowel *is* a separate syllable; e.g., *responsible* should be divided *responsi-ble*; the third syllable is *si*, not *i*.)

> typ-ical *not* typi-cal
> afford-able *not* afforda-ble
> inexhaust-ible *not* inexhausti-ble
> cler-ical *not* cleri-cal
> suit-able *not* suita-ble

7. Divide hyphenated compound words at the hyphen connecting the parts of the compound.

> self-confidence *not* self-confi-dence
> random-access *not* random-ac-cess
> eye-catching *not* eye-catch-ing

Divide unhyphenated compounds between the parts of the word.

> business-people *not* busi-nesspeo-ple
> weather-proof *not* weath-erproof

8. Avoid dividing the last word of consecutive lines.

9. Avoid dividing the final word of a paragraph or page.

10. Do not divide figures or abbreviations.

> $625,000 *not* $625,-000
> **YMCA** *not* **YM-CA**

11. If you must place the parts of a name or a name and a title on different lines, make the division so that interpretation will be as easy as possible.

Mrs. Joanne M./ Cotroneo *not* Mrs./ Joanne/ M. Cotroneo
Albert/ Meier, M.D. *not* Albert Meier,/ M.D.
Grand/ Rapids *not* Grand Rap/-ids

12. If you cannot place an entire address on the same line, present the parts as shown below.

1529 East/ Oak Street *not* 1529/ East Oak/ Street
418 Sims/ Boulevard *not* 418/ Sims Boulevard
Midland,/ Texas *not* Mid-/ land, Texas
San Francisco,/ California *not* San/ Francisco, California
Elgin,/ IL 60123-9998 *not* Elgin, IL/ 60123-9998

13. If you cannot place all parts of a date on the same line, divide between the day and the year, not between the month and the day.

June 13,/ 19-- *not* June/ 13, 19--

CHECK YOUR UNDERSTANDING 78

Rewrite the following expressions. Using a diagonal to show the end of a line, indicate the most appropriate dividing point, if any, in each expression. Write *no* after expressions you should not divide.

prize-winning	M.B.A.
September 5, 19--	Cedar Rapids, Iowa
Mr. Otto R. Crest	9218 South Parker Avenue
Grants Pass, Oregon	Ms. Christine R. Parga
$433,615	user-friendly

 EDITING APPLICATIONS

1. Using hyphens as appropriate and a diagonal to show the end of a line, indicate the appropriate dividing points, if any, in each of the following expressions. Write *no* after expressions you should not divide.

   a. Ms. Nadine L. Goldblatt
   b. using
   c. $248,630
   d. photographer
   e. likable
   f. hasn't
   g. shopping
   h. Miss Leni Redmon
   i. thirty-seven
   j. 2944 North Greenville Parkway
   k. comprehensible
   l. escape
   m. beautiful
   n. Miss Gayle Cruce
   o. reconciliation
   p. dwelling
   q. insurable
   r. 16 East Weatherford Drive
   s. international
   t. knowledge
   u. Sante Fe, New Mexico
   v. $873.35
   w. debatable
   x. Dr. Gordon M. Lorch
   y. substantial
   z. father-in-law
   aa. YWCA
   bb. dependable
   cc. reproduce
   dd. radio
   ee. North Platte, Nebraska
   ff. buzzing
   gg. proceeded
   hh. Great Falls, Montana
   ii. proprietary
   jj. resistible
   kk. Greensboro, NC 27420-4136
   ll. represent
   mm. straight
   nn. occurrence

SECTION V

Common Letter Formats

Effective letters that make a good impression have the following qualities:

- Attractive format and appearance
- Accurate spelling, punctuation, word choice, and grammar
- Clear organization and complete information

When keying a letter, visualize each page and balance the keyed material and the white space. Select margins with reference to the length of the letter so that each page has an uncrowded, balanced look. Leave side margins of 1 to 2 inches and a bottom margin of at least 1 inch. See Table V-1, page 141, for detailed information about letter placement.

If your company has an official format for correspondence, follow that format.

Illustrations V-2 and V-5 on pages 142-145 show common letter formats.

			TABLE V-1	LETTER PLACEMENT GUIDE	

Letter Classification	Words in Letter Body	Side Margins	Margin Settings		Date Position*
			Elite	Pica	
Short	Up to 100	2"	24-78	20-65	Line 18
Average	101-200	$1\frac{1}{2}$	18-84	15-70	Line 16
Long	201-300	1"	12-90	10-75	Line 14
Two-page	More than 300	1"	12-90	10-75	Line 14
Standard 6" line for all letters**	As above for all letters	$1\frac{1}{4}$"	15-87	12-72	As above for all letters

*If a deep letterhead prevents keying the date on the designated line, place the date a double space below the last line of the letterhead.

**Some companies use a standard 6" line for all letters. Use this placement only when so directed.

[1]Adapted from Jerry W. Robinson, et al., *Century 21 Keyboarding, Formatting, and Document Processing*, 5th ed. (Cincinnati: South-Western Publishing Co., 1992), p. 76.

ILLUSTRATION V-2

Creative Media, Inc.
4782 Jackson Avenue
Annapolis, MD   21401-9407
(301) 555-9872

June 12, 19--

International Products, Inc.
Attention Administrative Manager
295 Madison Boulevard
Corning, NY 14830-2086

Ladies and Gentlemen

Many companies use the block format shown in this letter. Notice
that all lines begin at the left margin. Not having to indent the
date, paragraphs, and closing lines saves valuable keyboarding
time.

Usually open punctuation is used with this format. With open
punctuation, no punctuation marks appear after the salutation or
complimentary close.

Because the block format eliminates some keyboarding, the use of
this format saves time, increases letter production rates, and
reduces costs.

Please call me at 555-7843 to discuss further the block format.

Sincerely

Paula R. Robards

Paula R. Robards
Communication Manager

mls

You may expect to receive our complimentary monthly newsletter.

Block Format with Open Punctuation

ILLUSTRATION V-3

Association for Adult Education
294 Crestview Road
Philadelphia, PA 19147-5634
(215) 555-6317

August 8, 19--

Mr. Joseph P. Jabaily
Director, Rollins Industries
712 Friendly Avenue
Saginaw, MI 48606-4208

Dear Mr. Jabaily

MODIFIED BLOCK FORMAT

The modified block format differs from the block format in that
the date and closing lines begin at horizontal center. This letter is arranged in modified block format with open punctuation.
You may also use mixed punctuation (a colon after the salutation
and a comma after the complimentary close) with the modified block
format.

Although beginning both the date and closing lines at horizontal
center helps increase production rates, many companies still place
these lines at different horizontal points. For example, some
companies center the date, others key the date to end at the right
margin, and others place the date in relation to some feature of
the letterhead. Some companies place the closing lines five
spaces left of center or key them to end approximately at the
right margin.

The popularity of the modified block format is difficult to understand since this format requires more keyboarding strokes than the
block format. Perhaps companies using the modified block format
have not seriously considered the increased production rates that
can be obtained by using other letter formats.

Sincerely yours

ASSOCIATION FOR ADULT EDUCATION

Tanya V. Chen

Tanya V. Chen, President

djh

pc Brenda Dunning

Modified Block Format with Open Punctuation

ILLUSTRATION V-4

CLAIRMONT COMMUNICATION SERVICE
2473 West 34th Street
New York, NY 10044-3275
(212) 555-3742

```
                              December 10, 19--


REGISTERED MAIL

Mrs. Lynn M. Hall, Director
National Textile Co.
One Robertson Drive
Elkton, MD  21921-9753

Dear Mrs. Hall:

          MODIFIED BLOCK FORMAT WITH INDENTED PARAGRAPHS

     Business letters are generally formatted on 8 1/2-by-11-inch
letterhead which gives the name, address, and telephone number of
the organization sending the letter.

     This letter is arranged in modified block format with five-
space paragraph indentions.  The line on which the date is placed
varies according to the length of the letter.  Less space is left
above the date of longer letters than of shorter letters.  The
first line of the inside address is keyed on the fourth line below
the date.

     Margins also vary according to the length of the letter.
Shorter letters are generally formatted with wider margins; longer
letters, with narrower margins.  However, some businesses use a
standard six-inch line for all letters.

     A pamphlet describing acceptable letter formats and placement
guidelines is enclosed.  Please call me at 555-9638 to discuss any
other questions.

                         Sincerely,



                         Calvin D. Franz
                         Administrative Assistant


drj

Enclosure

pc Walter T. Miller
```

Modified Block Format with Indented Paragraphs and Mixed Punctuation

ILLUSTRATION V-5

213 Bentley Boulevard
Phoenix, AZ 85029-6531
Dunhill Office Systems (602) 555-2942

March 16, 19--

ADMINISTRATIVE MANAGER
CREATIVE SOFTWARE INC
6391 BRADFORD AVENUE
BANGOR ME 04401-9753

SIMPLIFIED BLOCK LETTER FORMAT

Simplified block letters are arranged in a functional, efficient
format. This format is a block letter without a salutation or a
complimentary close. Other features include the following:

1. Key the date on line 12 so the letter address will show
through the window of a window envelope.

2. Key the letter address in capital letters with no punctuation.
Use uppercase and lowercase letters with punctuation if that is
the format of addresses stored in an electronic address file.

3. Key the subject line in capital letters or in uppercase and
lowercase letters a double space below the inside address.

4. Begin the body a double space below the subject line.

5. Key numbered items flush with the left margin.

6. Key the writer's name and title in capital letters or in
uppercase and lowercase letters a quadruple space below the body.

7. Key reference initials a double space below the signature line
and include the keyboarder's initials only.

8. Key copy and enclosure notations a double space below the reference initials.

9. Use standard length line for all letters. A six-inch line is
common.

Because the simplified block letter format saves many keystrokes
and motions, companies using this letter format save time and increase office productivity.

Lawrence Rios

LAWRENCE RIOS, INFORMATION CENTER MANAGER

rla

cc Miss Constance D. Piccora

Simplified Block Letter Format

SECTION W

Common Memorandum Formats

Memorandums are informal messages sent between officials or employees of the same company, usually on forms provided by the company. Like business letters, memos should be accurate, correct, concise, and courteous. The guidelines relating to the body of a business letter also generally apply to memos.

Illustrations W-1 and W-2 on pages 148 and 149 show common memorandum formats.

ILLUSTRATION W-1

$\not{A}$ **Addison Industries, Inc.**
MEMORANDUM

TO: Donna C. Orton, Corporate Legal Counselor

FROM: James K. Powell, Human Resources Manager *JKP*

DATE: June 7, 19--

SUBJECT: Absentee Policy

To encourage compliance with our new absentee policy, John McCollum has asked that you and I meet with the staffs of the following six departments:

Accounting
Information Systems
Marketing
Production
Research and Development
Shipping and Receiving

We should be prepared to explain the reasons for the new policy and to answer questions. A copy of the absentee policy and concerns of which John is aware are enclosed.

Please let me know by Friday, June 15, with which three departments you would prefer to meet.

If you have questions, please call me at 555-8735.

rlt

Enclosures: 2

pc John K. McCollum

Formal Memorandum

ILLUSTRATION W-2

June 7, 19--

Donna C. Orton, Corporate Legal Counselor

ABSENTEE POLICY

To encourage compliance with our new absentee policy, John
McCollum has asked that you and I meet with the staffs of the
following six departments:

Accounting
Information Systems
Marketing
Production
Research and Development
Shipping and Receiving

We should be prepared to explain the reasons for the new policy
and to answer questions. A copy of the absentee policy and concerns of which John is aware are enclosed.

Please let me know by Friday, June 15, with which three departments you would prefer to meet.

If you have questions, please call me at 555-8735.

JKP

James K. Powell, Human Resources Manager

rlt

Enclosures: 2

pc John K. McCollum

Simplified Memorandum

SECTION X

Guidelines for Keying Footnotes and Bibliographies

Many business reports use footnotes and bibliographies. A **footnote** provides information that supplements the text. A **bibliography** lists sources used in preparing the report.

FOOTNOTES

Footnotes have the following purposes:

- To give credit for quotations or ideas taken from sources
- To refer readers to sources for additional information
- To provide explanations of interest to only a few readers

A footnote is most convenient when it is placed at the bottom of the page on which the quotation or borrowed idea appears. However, for ease of keyboarding or printing, footnotes are sometimes presented at the end of a section or chapter. Some word processing software will automatically place footnotes correctly at the bottom of appropriate pages.

Number footnotes consecutively through a short report. For reports or other works containing several chapters, begin renumbering footnotes with each new chapter.

A **footnote reference number** alerts readers to the fact that additional information is provided in a footnote. A footnote reference number should be placed in the following locations:

- Immediately after a statement to be explained in a footnote
- Immediately after a quotation to be identified in a footnote
- Immediately after a statement that introduces a table, chart, graph, or other material reproduced from a source

If you are placing footnotes at the bottom of the page on which the footnote reference number occurs, follow these guidelines in positioning the footnotes:

1. Allow room at the bottom of the page for all footnotes relating to that page.

2. After the last line of text on the page, double-space and key a 1 ½-inch divider line (using the underscore key), beginning at the left margin.

3. After keying the divider line, double-space and indent the reference number five spaces from the left margin.

4. Key the reference number one-half space above the line. (If using word processing software, insert the appropriate code.) Begin keying the footnote without spacing after the reference number.

5. Key the second and subsequent lines beginning at the left margin. Single-space the body of the footnote, but double-space between footnotes.

6. Leave at least a 1″ margin between the last footnote line and the bottom of the page.

Different firms use different styles for footnotes. However, the information contained in the footnotes should always be presented simply, clearly, and accurately. Furthermore, the sequence and punctuation of elements in footnotes should be consistent. Generally, the first reference to a source provides complete bibliographic information. Later references to the same source may be shortened. The model footnotes in Table X-1 (pages 152-155) illustrate first and later references for various sources in business reports.

TABLE X-1 FOOTNOTES	
Book (one author)	[1]Patricia M. Whalen, *Basic Skills for the Modern Office* (Cincinnati: South-Western Publishing Co., 1984), p. 33.
Later reference to same work in footnote 1, same page (no other works by same author cited previously)	[2]Whalen, p. 33.

TABLE X-1 CONTINUED	
Later reference to same work in footnote 1, same page (another work by same author cited previously)	[3]Whalen, *Basic Skills for the Modern Office*, p. 33.
Later reference to same work in footnote 1, different page (another work by same author cited previously)	[4]Whalen, *Basic Skills for the Modern Office*, p. 141.
Book (two authors)	[5]Patsy J. Fulton and Joanna D. Hanks, *Procedures for the Professional Secretary* (Cincinnati: South-Western Publishing Co., 1985), p. 74.
Later reference to footnote immediately preceding	[6]Ibid., p. 77.
Book (three authors)	[7]Jules Harcourt, A. C., "Buddy" Krizan, Patricia Merrier, *Business Communication* (Cincinnati: South-Western Publishing Co., 1987), p. 412.
Later reference to same work in footnote 7, different page*	[8]Harcourt, Krizan, and Merrier, p. 168.
Book (four or more authors)	[9]C. H. Duncan *et al.*, *College Keyboarding/Typewriting* (Cincinnati: South-Western Publishing Co., 1985), p. 105.
Later reference to same work in footnote 9, different page*	[10]Duncan *et al.*, p. 75.
Edited work	[11]Margaret P. Gregory and Wanda Daniel (eds.), *National Business Education Yearbook, No. 25* (Reston, Virginia: National Business Education Association, 1987) p. 134.
Later reference to same work in footnote 11, different page*	[12]Gregory and Daniel, p.71.
Multivolume Work	[13]R. H. Campbell and A. S. Skinner (eds.), *An Inquiry into the Nature and Causes of the*

TABLE X-1   CONTINUED

	Wealth of Nations (Indianapolis, IN: Liberty Classics, 1981), I, 31.
Later reference to same work in footnote 13, different page*	[14]Campbell and Skinner (eds.), I, 371.
Yearbook article	[15]Evelyn E. Harvey, "Human Relations Skills for the Changing Office," *Business Education for a Changing World*, edited by Margaret P. Gregory and Wanda Daniel. (Reston, Virginia: National Business Education Association, 1987), p. 30.
Later reference to same work in footnote 15, different page*	[16]Harvey, p. 33.
Signed encyclopedia article	[17]Frank Barron, "Creativity," *Encyclopaedia Britannica* (Chicago: Encyclopaedia Britannica, Inc., 1968), VI, p. 711.
Later reference to same work in footnote 17, different page*	[18]Barron, VI, p. 712
Unsigned encyclopedia article	[19]"Transit Circle," *Encyclopaedia Britannica* (1968), XXII, 171.
Later reference to same work in footnote 19, different page*	[20]"Transit Circle," XXII, p. 172.
Signed periodical article	[21]Georgina L. Seals, "Computers Enhance Learning through Networked System," *Business Education Forum*, Vol. XLII, No. 6 (March, 1988), p. 17.
Later reference to same work in footnote 21, different page*	[22]Seals, p. 15.
Unsigned periodical article	[23]"Job Hunting in Year 2000: Pointers to Consider," *The Secretary*, Vol. XLVIII, No. 3 (March, 1987), p. 6.
Signed newspaper article	[24]Jim Mitchell, "Southwestern Bell Reaches Out with Cautious Strategy," *The Dallas Morning News*, May 29, 1988 Section H, p. 1.

TABLE X-1 CONTINUED	
Unsigned newspaper article	[25]"Plans for Airplane-launched Rocket Reported," *The Dallas Morning News*, May 29, 1988, Section A, p. 3.
Unsigned Report	[26]*SFN Annual Report for Fiscal Year Ended April 30, 1983*, (Glenview, IL: SFN Companies, Inc., 1983), p. 4.
Unpublished dissertation	[27]Mary Louise Murriel, "An Investigation of Relationships of Performance, Learning Style, and Focus of Control Among Students in Postsecondary Word Processing Instruction," (Doctoral dissertation, Northern Illinois University, 1986), p. 3.
Later reference to same work in footnote 27, different page*	[28]Murriel, p. 5.

*If there is another work by the same author cited previously, include the title of the work to which you are referring as shown in footnotes 3 and 4.

BIBLIOGRAPHIES

A report that relies on source materials should provide a list of those materials. This list is called a **bibliography**.

To prepare a bibliography, arrange in alphabetical order a list of the sources you have used in preparing the report. This list should include materials to which you have referred in footnotes and all other materials used in writing the report.

Alphabetize the list according to the last name of the author (use the first author's name if there is more than one). If the work is unsigned, alphabetize the work according to the first important word in the title.

The forms for footnotes and for items in a bibliography differ. In a bibliography give the last name of an author first because items are alphabetized on that basis. In contrast, in a footnote give the first name, middle initial, and last name of an author in that order.

Other differences involve spacing and punctuation. In a bibliography, begin the first line of an entry in a bibliography at the margin and indent second and any additional lines five spaces. In contrast, indent the first line of a footnote five spaces beginning with a reference number keyed a half space above the line.

For two or more entries by the same author, give the author's name for the first entry only. Indicate omission of the name by keying in place of the name seven hyphens followed by a period. See the entries under *Whalen, Patricia M.,* in the model bibliographic entries in Table X-2 (pages 156-157).

The model bibliographic entries in Table X-2 include the same works that have been cited in the model footnotes. You can compare any bibliographic entry with the footnote reference to that work. In preparing a bibliography, follow in detail the format, contents, and punctuation for each type of entry.

TABLE X-2   BIBLIOGRAPHIC ENTRIES

Signed encyclopedia article	Barron, Frank. "Creativity," *Encyclopaedia Britannica,* VI, 711-712. Chicago: Encyclopaedia Britannica, Inc., 1968.
Book (four or more authors)	Duncan, C. H., *et al. College Keyboarding/Typewriting.* Cincinnati: South-Western Publishing Co., 1985.
Multivolume work	Campbell, R. H., and A. S. Skinner (eds.). *An Inquiry into the Nature and Causes of the Wealth of Nations.* 2 vols. Indianapolis, IN: Liberty Classics, 1981.
Book (two authors)	Fulton, Patsy J., and Joanna D. Hanks. *Procedures for the Professional Secretary.* Cincinnati: South-Western Publishing Co., 1985.
Edited Work	Gregory, Margaret P., and Wanda Daniel (eds.). *National Business Education Yearbook.* Reston, Virginia: National Business Education Association, 1987.
Book (three authors)	Harcourt, Jules, A. C. "Buddy" Krizan, and Patricia Merrier. *Business Communication.* Cincinnati: South-Western Publishing Co., 1987.

TABLE X-2   CONTINUED

Yearbook article	Harvey, Evelyn E. "Human Relations Skills for the Changing Office," *Business Education for the Changing World*, edited by Margaret P. Gregory and Wanda Daniel. Reston, Virginia: National Business Education Association, 1987, pp. 29-39.
Unsigned periodical article	"Job Hunting in Year 2000: Pointers to Consider." *The Secretary*, Vol. XLVIII, No. 3 (March, 1987), p. 6.
Signed newspaper article	Mitchell, Jim. "Southwestern Bell Reaches Out with Cautious Strategy." *The Dallas Morning News*, May 29, 1988, Section H, p. 1.
Unpublished Dissertation	Murriel, Mary Louise. "An Investigation of Relationships of Performance, Learning Style, and Focus of Control Among Students in Postsecondary Word Processing Instruction." Doctoral dissertation, Northern Illinois University, 1986.
Unsigned newspaper article	"Plans for Airplane-launched Rocket Reported." *The Dallas Morning News*, May 29, 1988, Section A, p. 3.
Signed periodical article	Seals, Georgina L. "Computers Enhance Learning through Networked System." *Business Education Forum*, Vol. XLII, No. 6 (March, 1988), pp. 15-17.
Unsigned Report	*SFN Annual Report for Fiscal Year Ended April 30, 1983*. Glenview, IL: SFN Companies, Inc., 1983.
Unsigned encyclopedia article	"Transit Circle," *Encyclopaedia Britannica* (1968), XXII, pp. 171-172.
Book (one author)	Whalen, Patricia M. *Basic Skills for the Modern Office*. Cincinnati: South-Western Publishing Co., 1984.
Second entry by Whalen	———. *Manual for Basic Skills for the Modern Office*. Cincinnati: South-Western Publishing Co., 1984.

SECTION Y

Abbreviations

Use capitalized two-letter state abbreviations (without periods) and ZIP codes for addresses in the United States. Also, use capitalized two-letter province abbreviations for addresses in Canada.

U.S. State/District/Territory Abbreviations

Alabama	AL	Montana	MT
Alaska	AK	Nebraska	NE
Arizona	AZ	Nevada	NV
Arkansas	AR	New Hampshire	NH
California	CA	New Jersey	NJ
Colorado	CO	New Mexico	NM
Connecticut	CT	New York	NY
Delaware	DE	North Carolina	NC
District of Columbia	DC	North Dakota	ND
Florida	FL	Ohio	OH
Georgia	GA	Oklahoma	OK
Guam	GU	Oregon	OR
Hawaii	HI	Pennsylvania	PA
Idaho	ID	Puerto Rico	PR
Illinois	IL	Rhode Island	RI
Indiana	IN	South Carolina	SC
Iowa	IA	South Dakota	SD
Kansas	KS	Tennessee	TN
Kentucky	KY	Texas	TX
Louisiana	LA	Utah	UT
Maine	ME	Vermont	VT
Maryland	MD	Virginia	VA
Massachusetts	MA	Virgin Islands	VI
Michigan	MI	Washington	WA
Minnesota	MN	West Virginia	WV
Mississippi	MS	Wisconsin	WI
Missouri	MO	Wyoming	WY

Canadian Province Abbreviations

Alberta	AB	Nova Scotia	NS
British Columbia	BC	Ontario	ON
Manitoba	MB	Prince Edward Island	PE
New Brunswick	NB	Newfoundland	NF
Quebec	PQ	Northwest Territories	NT
Saskatchewan	SK	Yukon Territory	YT

USEFUL BUSINESS ABBREVIATIONS

From time to time, you must use abbreviations of business terms on forms and in statistical materials. However, avoid using abbreviations in business correspondence.

Some of the most common business abbreviations are the following:

account	acct.
accounts payable	AP
accounts receivable	AR
also known as	a.k.a.
amount	amt.
as soon as possible	ASAP
association	assn.
attachment	att.
average	avg. or av.
Bachelor of Arts	B.A.
Bachelor of Science	B.S.
balance	bal.
cash (or collect) on delivery	c.o.d.
Celsius or centigrade	C
centimeter	cm
certified public accountant	CPA
Certified Professional Secretary	CPS
chief executive officer	CEO
corporation	corp.
credit	cr.
department	dept.
district	dist.
each	ea.
enclosure	enc.
end of month	EOM
esquire	Esq.
estimated time of arrival	ETA
et cetera, and so forth	etc.
Fahrenheit	F

Federal Deposit Insurance Corporation	FDIC
first in, first out	FIFO
fiscal year	FY
foot, feet	ft.
for example	e.g.
for your information	FYI
free on board	f.o.b.
gram	g
gross	gr.
Gross National Product	GNP
headquarters	hdqrs.
incorporated	inc.
insurance	ins.
international	intl.
kilogram	kg
kilometer	km
liter	L
last in, first out	LIFO
limited	Ltd. or ltd.
Master of Business Administration	M.B.A.
manufacturing	mfg.
maximum	max.
merchandise	mdse.
meter	m
miles per gallon	mpg
miles per hour	mph
milligram	mg
millimeter	mm
net in 60 days	$^{n}/_{60}$
net weight	nt. wt.
not applicable	NA
number	no.
numbers	nos.
package	pkg.
page	pg. or p.
pages	pp.
paid	pd.
pound	lb.
quantity	qty.
quarter	qtr.
received	recd.
Reply, if you please	R.S.V.P.
revolutions per minute	rpm

Securities Exchange Commission	SEC
that is	i.e.
vice president	VP
volume	vol.
week	wk.
weight	wt.

SECTION Z

Parliamentary Procedure

Parliamentary procedure is a set of rules used to conduct formal meetings. Parliamentary procedure allows meeting participants to express viewpoints and to make decisions without confusion.

OBJECTIVES

The objectives of parliamentary procedure are the following:

- To expedite meetings
- To maintain order
- To ensure justice and equality for all
- To assist groups in accomplishing their purposes

When an organization is formed, written guidelines—called **bylaws**—are established that will help govern the organization. Bylaws include at least the following information: the name of the organization, the group's objective, the qualifications for members, the officers' titles and duties, the regular meeting dates, the composition of the executive board, the types of committees, the authority for parliamentary procedure, and the method for amending the bylaws.

COMMON VOCABULARY

To understand parliamentary procedures, you must know the common vocabulary:

Ad hoc committees—special committees
Adjourn—to end a meeting
Agenda—an outline of the order of business
Amend—to change the wording of a motion or a resolution
Announcement—a notification presented for the group's information (The Chairperson may make or call upon other officers or members to make any necessary announcements.)

Assembly—the group having the meeting
Chairperson—the presiding officer
Discussion—oral consideration of a motion or question by the group
Division of the assembly—the motion that calls for the people to stand to vote
Ex officio—members of the group because of the position they hold (Ex officio members usually do not have voting privileges.)
Floor—recognition from the presiding officer for permission to speak
General consent—silent consent without an objection
Main motion—a motion which introduces a topic to the group
Majority vote—more than half of the eligible votes
Minutes—written report of the happenings at a meeting
Motion—proposal for the members to discuss (To make a motion, a person should say; I move that . . . .")
New business—matters initiated at the present meeting (i.e., business not previously discussed by the group)
Objection—an objection enables the group to avoid considering a motion the group feels should not come before the assembly
Old business—business continued from a previous meeting
Pending question—the motion which has been stated by the Chairperson and is being discussed by the group
Pro Tem—the one who serves in the absence of the chairperson or person in charge
Quorum—the minimum number of members who must be present so the group may have a meeting (It is a majority of all members in the group unless stated differently by the bylaws.)
Special committees—committees established to accomplish specified tasks (i.e., ad hoc committees)
Standing committees—permanent committees
Standing rules—rules that temporarily replace parliamentary procedure
Stating the question—restatement of the motion by the Chairperson
Tellers—persons designated to count votes or written ballots
Vote—expression of opinion or choice (either positive or negative)
Withdraw a motion—to remove a motion from consideration (A motion must be withdrawn by the person who made the motion.)

TYPICAL MEETING PROCEDURE

Organizations that use parliamentary procedure follow a fixed order of business outlined on an **agenda**. A typical meeting proceeds as follows:

1. CALL TO ORDER

   The Chairperson says, "The meeting will come to order."

2. READING AND APPROVAL OF THE MINUTES

   The Chairperson says, "The secretary will read the minutes of the last meeting." After the secretary reads the minutes, the chairperson says, "Are there any corrections to the minutes? (pause) If there are no (further) corrections, the minutes stand approved as read (as corrected)."

3. OFFICERS' REPORTS

   Usually, only the treasurer reports. After the report is presented by the treasurer, the Chairperson asks: "Are there any questions about the treasurer's report?" When all questions have been answered satisfactorily, the Chairperson says, "The treasurer's report will be placed on file for audit."

4. COMMITTEE REPORTS

   The Chairperson asks for reports from the chairpersons of the standing committees (permanent committees) and any special committees (ad hoc committees). The Chairperson should know in advance which committees have reports to deliver.

5. ANNOUNCEMENTS

   The Chairperson says "Are there any announcements?"

6. OLD BUSINESS

   The Chairperson *does not* ask for old business. He or she automatically mentions items that were postponed from the previous meeting or that were not concluded at the previous meeting.

7. NEW BUSINESS

   The Chairperson says, "Is there any new business?" Each topic that is raised must be disposed of before a new topic is considered.

8. ANNOUNCEMENT OF NEXT MEETING

   The Chairperson indicates when the next meeting will be held.

9. ADJOURNMENT

   The Chairperson says, "Is there any further business? (pause) If not, the meeting will adjourn. (pause) The meeting is adjourned."

   To find out more about other aspects of parliamentary procedure, refer to the current edition of *Robert's Rules of Order, Newly Revised*.

INDEX